THE GAME MASTER'S HANDBOOK OF

PROACTIVE ROLEPLAYING

GUIDELINES AND STRATEGIES FOR RUNNING
PC-DRIVEN NARRATIVES IN 5E ADVENTURES

✳ JONAH AND TRISTAN FISHEL ✳

FOREWORD
BY GINNY DI

AFTERWORD
BY JEFF ASHWORTH

ILLUSTRATIONS BY
LUKE EIDENSCHINK

DEDICATION

To the Friday Knights, my brothers-in-arms, for exploring many worlds with me. And to Sarah, for rolling the dice on me.

-JF

To my loyal group for putting up with years of adventures, struggling through laggy video calls or standing around a rickety table. Thank you for putting up with my shenanigans, and I thank you for your own.

-TF

THE GAME MASTER'S HANDBOOK OF PROACTIVE ROLEPLAYING

CONTENTS

FOREWORD

AS SOMEONE WHO PROFESSIONALLY CREATES instructional tabletop gaming content dedicated to helping both players and Game Masters focus on story and character, I take great pride in allowing players to explore their own character arcs—so you can imagine the shock I felt when I first read this book and realized I was still doing it all wrong.

I've always put a lot of effort into weaving my players' character goals and backstories into the larger plot arc of the campaign. After all, they're supposed to be the heroes! They shouldn't just be pursuing the overall game narrative; their own narratives should feel intrinsically tied to that story. When starting a new game, it's not unusual for me to lie awake at night, obsessively picking at plot threads so I can tie everything together in a way that makes my players into collaborators instead of onlookers.

But Jonah and Tristan Fishel radically changed my understanding of tabletop narrative within just a few pages of this book. Before I even reached the first chapter, I understood that I could be delivering a more personal, more engaging story to my players while simultaneously diminishing my workload as a Game Master. In short, I had been cutting firewood with a pocketknife, and the authors of this book had just handed me a greataxe.

In the following pages, you will learn the fundamental flaws built into the most widely-accepted structure for heroic storytelling—and how to dismantle this structure in your own games. Case studies from the authors' own sessions demonstrate how to put their instruction into practice, and templates and charts offer easy-to-follow guidance for your own games. By the end, you will know how to guide your players to create proactive characters and how to create a world that reacts to their choices with compelling obstacles and challenges.

Finally, if you're anything like me, you will find yourself reevaluating the role of the Game Master entirely—making way for a game that will be more satisfying for everyone at the table.

Ginny Di
RPG Author, YouTuber, Cosplayer and Elf-Ear Enthusiast

INTRODUCTION

THE DARK LORD rises in the east and a fellowship comes together to stop him.

Another Dark Lord returns to life in the north, and a slightly different fellowship comes together in order to stop him, but this time only women know magic.

A totally different Dark Lord emerges (this time he's in space) and helps build a galaxy-spanning empire and a planet-destroying weapon, and a plucky band of rebels and space wizards come together to overthrow him and the emperor who controls his fate.

We all know these stories. They're classics of the fantasy genre, and, along with their characters, have come to define the tropes of that genre and because early tabletop roleplaying games took place in fantasy settings, they have had a direct influence on the games we play.

They also follow a predictable pattern: The evil guys do something and the good guys do something to stop them. In many of these stories, "good" is only defined as "acting against evil." The protagonists are mostly reactive—they make choices based on the antagonist's choices, the literary equivalent of Newton's Third Law of Motion.

If you try to think of other examples of this "good reacts to evil" trope, you'll probably be able to think of more than you can keep track of, even if you limit yourself to the realms of classic fantasy. Once you get to more modern incarnations—superhero stories, for example—this pattern becomes even more obvious: the bad guy turns half the universe to dust with the snap of his fingers and the good guys have to assemble a team to go back in time to stop him; the Dark Lord forges a massively powerful weapon and the races of Middle Earth must join forces to stop him; A dragon has taken up residence in a once-great underground city, and the good guys must venture below to defeat him.

Let us be clear: This isn't a bad thing. Good rallying against evil is the bedrock of fantasy. It sets the stakes, places obstacles and opportunities for growth in the path of the characters and creates some juicy conflict to explore. From a storytelling perspective, it's a tried-and-true approach that works well for the genre. In short, it works.

Game Masters for tabletop roleplaying games have inherited this same reactive plot structure through the genealogy of our fantasy tabletop games. Unfortunately, having our protagonists be only reactive is not always a fun way to play or run a game. In sum? It doesn't work.

THE GENEALOGY OF FANTASY TTRPGS

The most popular tabletop roleplaying games in the world can trace most of their thematic DNA to Gary Gygax and his grognard friends, who were steeped in the works of Tolkien and its derivatives. Just as the wargaming roots of Gygax's original game gave rise to the combat-heavy, action-packed rule set of Dungeons & Dragons, the classic fantasy setting of their games gave rise to our modern "reactive fantasy" TTRPGs.

Reactive fantasy in a wargaming setting makes a lot of sense: There is a bad guy (or girl, or nebulous, genderless entity), and the party is good, so they should fight back. Let's break out the battle mats and roll some dice! But as Game Masters, always framing our stories and adventures in terms of antagonists acting and protagonists reacting limits the scope of the stories we can tell.

First, reactive roleplay places most of the creative responsibility on you, the Game Master. You must always think about what the forces you've created have in store for the world, while also presenting enough quest hooks and loot drops to ensure your party actually tries to stop the end of the world (read: reacting). For many Game Masters, this part of the game is a lot of fun, and designing engaging fantasy worlds and intriguing non-player characters might be why they got into GMing in the first place. But relying on the Game Master to drive the entire game fosters bad habits in players—they start to assume the story will come to them, that the GM will always present them with something to react to, that their actions will ultimately save the day even if they refuse to go into the dungeon and slay the dragon that wants to eat the world.

It also limits a Game Master's creativity. If all of our material follows the same pattern and the players are bound to react to it in the same ways, we fall into a creative rut. We run the same stories over and over again and only occasionally swap the paint (on the story beats. And the minis). This repetitive cycle is the biggest enemy of fun—after all, if you always know what's coming next, how can you ever be surprised?

Finally, the reactive approach robs players of the agency that differentiates TTRPGs from other forms of gameplay. In fact, in a reactive fantasy game, character creation is the only stage of the game in which the players have true agency. After that, their characters ultimately must choose from among the options the Game Master gives them during the campaign, limited by the "stop the big bad evil guy from doing the evil plan" story beats. Running a game in which the players are always reacting to the material presented by the Game Master limits the effect a player can have on the world of the game. And suddenly, another campaign of heroic reactions feels a lot less fun than saying:

"Let's Try an Evil Campaign!"

Most Game Masters have heard this phrase in some form before. There's something seductive about running an "evil" campaign, in which players bring despicable characters to life and are free to let their twisted impulses run free. When your game has hit a creative rut, the players are disconnected, maybe even frustrated with the game and the appeal of walking away from saving the world so you can instead become a powerful lich king who can create worlds of his own is apparent. We've both played in and run evil campaigns, and you know what? They're actually super fun.

You know what they aren't? Reactive. Evil campaigns are never framed in the same reactive way as traditional good campaigns. Evil campaigns never start with "the lawful good priest is preparing a holy ritual to heal all the sick in the town, and you must muster your dark forces to stop him." They start with, "OK, let's do some evil—what did you have in mind?" and then the players rush off on some wild and/ or misguided scheme to take over the world.

Notice the difference between this kind of campaign and a

traditional game: In this context, the players have some ideas in mind for the dastardly acts they want to commit, then they pursue them. They expect the game world to react to them instead of the other way around. In the best evil campaigns, the typical script is flipped entirely: The players are the ones making the evil schemes and causing reactive heroes to rise up to stop them (only to be crushed!).

These campaigns are fun not because—well, not only because— you're playing evil characters, but because you are playing proactively instead of reactively. The encounters put in your way by the Game Master are the logical consequences of your actions, not predetermined story beats and evil plots to foil. The game takes on an entirely different tone, and players get excited to cook up new plots and expand on their old ones.

This isn't a feature unique to evil games: It's a symptom of something deeper. In classic fantasy, evil is the proactive force and good is the reactive force. In fact, in nearly all classic fantasy, evil is the change-inducing, world-shaping force and good is the status quo-preserving, conservative force.

When players are focused on disrupting the status quo as part of an evil campaign, they think about what their characters want, strategize on how to get there and then gleefully blow through all the barriers the Game Master puts in their way. This pattern is a blast to play and a blast to run since the fun is baked into the fundamental premise instead of being something we add in through roleplay gimmicks, clever monster mechanics or challenging boss fights. But you don't have to encourage evil-doing to play a proactive game. You just have to set things up a bit differently to achieve...

PROACTIVE PLAY IN A NON-EVIL GAME

The first time we noticed the difference between reactive and proactive play was during a game that was a full 180 from our usual swords and sorcery systems. The TTRPG Blades in the Dark is about too many things to mention here, but one of the things it's about is a crew of scoundrels trying to make it in the criminal underworld of a dark fantasy city.

In the Blades campaign we ran and played in, characters formed their own goals, negotiated with each other about priorities and got themselves into and out of trouble over and over again. It was a remarkably easy game to run—it simply wrote itself. Even when faced with a traditional "evil rises" plot point in the form of a waking Lovecraftian demon, the party simply absorbed that demon into their plans, extorted it, double-crossed it, then bargained their way back into its good graces for the low, low price of their mortal souls. The big bad evil guy became just another arrow in their quiver, a vehicle they could use in pursuit of their own goals.

This dynamic was an absolute joy to play, and the sheer fun of that game is something we still talk about. As the campaign unfolded, we realized the game was fun because the players were playing proactively, deciding what they wanted to do and going after it in their own way and in their own time. Jonah's role as the Game Master was to facilitate the fun, not invent it out of whole cloth. It was much more enjoyable for everyone when we were free of the standard action + equal and opposite reaction formula.

We started to wonder if the same narrative-driven principles used in many indie games might be used in our more traditional tabletop fantasy games. Nearly all of the shorter traditional campaigns we had run, and all the longer traditional campaigns, had followed a structure of coming together to stop some great evil plot. All of these games felt very different to us at the time, but looking back, they were all similar, even when we consciously tried to innovate. We wondered, could we encourage our players to behave proactively and make our role the facilitation of fun? Or, would the traditional fantasy setting seep into the game and make that kind of play impossible? We had assumed it would be the latter. We were wrong.

In the end, creating a structure for our players to take the lead was laughably easy. We were able to involve the players in some key planning processes, collaborate on some engaging character goals and then build a simple campaign start. From there, the experimental proactive campaign took off, with players actively pursuing the things they were interested in and constantly pushing the boundaries of the world we had created. They sought out things that were interesting to them, dealt with the consequences of their actions and pursued power and justice in a traditional fantasy setting with the same zeal the players in the Blades group had pursued high crimes and misdemeanors.

We weren't even doing anything radically different. In fact, all the Game Mastering tools we needed were already in our kit. We still approached running the game with roughly the same set of behaviors and practices for creating and playing NPCs, monsters, locations and rewards as we always did—we just reorganized them around the central theme of encouraging proactive play and discouraging reactive play. Once we made that mental shift and organized our prep time around it, everything fell into place.

All the things that make a tabletop game fun are natural parts of proactive play, and many things that make tabletop games boring are a natural part of reactive play. By intentionally designing our game around the principle of proactive play, encouraging players to design their own goals (within the limits we collectively set) and pursue them in a way that's fun for them, we transform the game into something that feels exciting, new and dynamic.

THE BENEFITS OF A PROACTIVE FANTASY GAME

That proactive fantasy game is ongoing, and it is with the goal of sharing that game's magic that we are writing this guidebook. In our thousands of hours of Game Mastering, we have learned a great deal about how to keep players engaged and interested. Since our reactive versus proactive epiphany—at least 1,000 hours spent running games—we began to apply that knowledge to a new goal: encouraging proactive play. Which is, ultimately, why this book got written in the first place.

Switching our games to proactive roleplaying transforms the way we feel and think about playing. Since we aren't responsible for providing all of the story for the group, we can spend more time creating exciting encounters and memorable NPCs. The change pushed our groups out of creative ruts and introduced a new sense of wonder to our games since the responsibility of moving the plot forward lies with the players and no one is sure how things will turn out. Finally, it changed our game's culture from one where we told the stories and the players observed to one where we all explored and discovered the story of our game together.

Reframing your game in this way helps codify all your scattered Game Master best practices into a cohesive set of fun-oriented principles that will transform the way you run your sessions. We've collected all our tips and tricks here and connected them to the theory of proactive play in a way that makes them easy to introduce to your own campaign. Our hope is that you take what you find useful here and apply it to your table in a way that makes sense to you and your players.

Running Your Own Proactive Fantasy Game

Now that we're through the why of this book, we'll spend the rest of our time talking about the how. To ensure a proactive approach in your own Game Mastering, you'll need to establish two rules:

1. Players must set goals for their characters that they can pursue in the world of the game. These goals will form the substance of your game and may change over time as players accomplish them and form new ones in response to how the world and their characters change.

2. You must facilitate the pursuit of the players' goals by setting obstacles and challenges in their way and by rewarding them for accomplishing their goals.

Everything we talked about above flows naturally from these two roles: the players as the drivers of the action and you as the facilitator of the world. The players will decide what they want to do and how they plan to pursue it; you will decide and track how the world reacts to those best laid plans.

The Responsibilities of the Players

Players in a proactive fantasy game are responsible for driving the plot forward and deciding where the game will go. The character goals the players create will dictate which encounters and adventures the players find during the campaign. The players are also responsible for playing through those encounters honestly with the intention of discovering what will happen to their character, not deciding it. The fun of tabletop games is that the most important outcomes are decided by the numbers on the dice, not the players or GM.

The players are also responsible for developing new goals as they continue their adventures. The creative part of the game doesn't stop at character creation as it typically does in the old reactive format—players are responsible for deciding how their characters will act in a given situation (Goal: claim the treasure hoard of a powerful and tyrannical dragon for themselves), how they will accomplish their goals (Plan: enlist the help of a legendary but retired blacksmith to forge the perfect dragon-slaying weapon to confront the beast) and the new goals they will establish after the world reacts to their actions (Goal: defend their hard-won gold from the horde of marauding orcs pouring out of the mountains).

The Responsibilities of the Game Master

In a proactive fantasy game, the Game Master is responsible for facilitating the fun, not providing it. The players provide the content and the goals, and the Game Master decides how to turn these goals into unforgettable encounters. To begin, they need to create or present a setting. But after the players have created characters with goals that fit that setting and engage with it in interesting ways, it is the Game Master's responsibility to fill in the details of the world in a way that responds to player goals, rather than telling a predetermined story. Most of all, the Game Master is responsible for creating encounters that represent the obstacles the game world presents to the characters as they pursue their goals.

The Game Master is also responsible for the behind-the-scenes accounting of the game, the goals and plots of villains and NPCs and the capabilities and resources of factions. Every Game Master has a preference for how closely to track these things, but no matter how granular you get, tracking this information is essential because you'll need to know the state of the world in order to decide which obstacles will stand in the way of the characters as they pursue their goals.

CREATING THE WORLD

The best way to get your group on board with a proactive game is to make your game collaborative from the very beginning: The initial creation of your fantasy world should not be the sole responsibility of the Game Master.

The fantasy world your group chooses to play in determines the tone of the game you want to play. A decision this central to the tone and culture of your table needs to be a group decision. Whatever method you choose to create your setting, it will benefit your table to

---

STOREBOUGHT OR HOMEBREWED?

You will notice that throughout this book, we assume that you are running adventures you've created in a world you've designed. That shouldn't stop you from applying this approach to established campaign settings or official sourcebooks or adventure modules.

---

choose together. Once the setting has been established, the players will have a clear idea of their character goals and the Game Master will have a clear idea of the kind of things they should prepare.

From there, you'll spend your time creating interesting locations, engaging NPCs and dramatic and narratively appropriate encounters. Your players will start to talk about what their characters want to do next. You'll start to hear players say "I" instead of "my character" as they get more invested in their character and the world around them. A powerful energy will fill your table, an energy that can only come from a group with a clear vision for the way forward and electric curiosity for how they will get there.

RUNNING A PROACTIVE GAME: A TIMELINE

The process for running most proactive games looks like this:

1. Create/choose the world or design/choose the setting that you'll be playing in with your group.

   a. Decide on the tone, ground rules and expectations.

   b. Decide on the character genre, or the range of genres, based on the world you're playing in.

   c. Fill out any details you need in order to create PCs.

2. Have players create characters (ideally together).

   a. Discuss the characters you will play and negotiate party roles (damage, control, support, etc.) for your game system.

   b. Create PC goals together (covered in the next chapter) with the oversight of the Game Master.

   c. Compare PC goals and identify reasons your characters might come together and cooperate on their early adventures.

3. Conceptualize your first few encounters.

   a. Identify groups of PC goals that either work well together (concerning the same location, NPCs or other plot device) or are opposed to one another (two claims to one item or location, conflicting ideologies, etc.).

   b. Talk to the players about the goals they'd like to pursue first, pointing out the groups of goals identified above. From here, schedule your first session.

   c. Based on the goals the players are likely to pursue first (and ideally have explicitly said they'll pursue first), think of the obstacles standing in their way. Think big and vague at first.

4. Fill in details around your first few encounters.

   a. Once you have an idea of the forces that will oppose your character goals, determine who directs those forces, where they are located and other details. Brainstorm with the players if you like.

   b. Stay general. Only think as far out as a mid-term goal at most. You can always retcon a particular place or person to be important for a long-term goal.

   c. Do as much prep as you prefer for these few encounters.

5. Play the game!

6. Run some post-game accounting.

   a. Based on the outcomes of the encounters (won, lost and the cost of each), have players re-examine their goals. If goals have been reached (or are no longer attainable), have players generate new ones.

   b. Some players may be inspired by play and want to formulate new goals for themselves, too. Encourage them!

   c. Based on the outcome of play, track any behind-the-scenes faction actions, location changes, NPC goals or any other effects you need to. For example, the players find a lost magic item: a faction might approach them and ask to take it.

7. Repeat Steps 3 through 7, starting with the new goals established in the old Step 6, as your game starts to take shape.

Notice how the structure laid out here is different from a traditional game, in which the Game Master decides on an event, the players react, then the Game Master changes the world according to their actions before deciding on a new event. That difference is everything.

Chapter 1

⸺✦·✧⸺

CHARACTER GOALS

FUN AND ENGAGING player character goals are the foundation upon which the rest of a proactive fantasy game is built: If your players don't have exciting and engaging goals to pursue in your game, then the game itself won't be as exciting or engaging. It's not incredibly difficult to come up with goals for characters, but it can be hard to ensure those goals are as engaging as they are challenging. This chapter is about setting the tone for your proactive fantasy games by encouraging your players to create compelling, achievable and satisfying goals. At the end of the chapter, you'll find a checklist to walk each of your players through so you can easily implement these concepts into your own game.

THE RESPONSIBILITY OF CHARACTER GOAL CREATION BELONGS TO THE PLAYERS

One more time for the people in the back: The responsibility for creating character goals falls to the players, not the Game Master. Players know what they'll enjoy playing and want to play, and it's an act of futility to tell them how to have fun. The Game Master's real job—facilitating the fun of the game—is much easier when the players have goals that align with each other's and the tone of the game your group wants to play.

Ensuring they do is also under the GM's purview.

For example, if your group wants to play a traditional swords and sorcery game in one of the many published settings for that type of thing, some of your players might come up with goals like "I want to discover a lost spell that will grant me the power of flight," "I want to destroy the tribe of orcs that killed my family" or "I want to convert the leader of the Cult of Shadows to the light of my god." A player with a less dramatic (but no less inspired) goal such as "I want to invent a delicious new way to eat meat, beans and cheese inside a corn flour shell" might fit into this group of players. Pursuing their goal and moving this plot forward might pull the other players away from their goals, but if the goal fits the tone of your game and the world you're creating, it will be entertaining for everyone. On the other hand, if your group expects the game to unfold with a more serious tone, Prometheus the Taco-Bringer should probably come up with a different goal.

Just as some goals don't align with established tone, other goals don't align with player cohesion. A player who comes to the table with the earnest character goal of "I want to steal the magic items of everyone else in the group" is a real pain to play with. A bit of conflict among the party can be a lot of fun, but not if one player's idea of a good time is ruining everyone else's opportunity to have one. In the aforementioned scenario, we'd likely ask the player if they could find another goal that would express the underhanded and shifty aesthetic of the character they want to play in a way that won't annoy or undercut other players.

While it is the player's responsibility to generate engaging character goals, it is the Game Master's responsibility to make sure those goals align with those of the rest of the group and with the type of game you want to play. If the players are new to this style of play, it's also your responsibility to guide them in creating character goals that adhere to the Rules of Proactive Fun. What are those? Glad you asked.

THE RULES OF PROACTIVE FUN

In a proactive fantasy game, players should be concerned with creating character goals they are compelled to pursue and complete. These should be the driving force of their individual character's efforts, but, more importantly, these should also be crucial and invigorating to the player. The more invested the player is in accomplishing their goal, the more likely they are to accomplish it (i.e., the more they'll want to show up and prepare for regular sessions). Not all the goals that players come up with are created equal: Some are much easier (and, as an added bonus, better) to build a game around. Here are the rules we recommend for players as they establish goals.

1. Each character should have multiple goals.

One goal is better than none, but three or four goals per player will activate your games in a way that ensures each session has at least one motivating force. These goals can be connected (a character who wants to be crowned the rightful monarch will first need to obtain the ceremonial garb of the kingdom and an army to enforce the claim) but should encompass or involve different things, allowing for different avenues of play if one quest needs to be put on hold for a while (if the ceremonial garb can't be stolen until a particular religious holiday that's months away, it's time to start raising an army in the meantime).

If a character insists on doing one thing and one thing only, it is easy for them (and the rest of you) to get stuck in a one-sided and much less interesting story. Goal diversity ensures there's always something to do. A single-minded character can still have multiple goals within one grand overarching objective, but the more varied their sub-goals are (like the throne-seeking character above), the easier the game will be to run.

A good number of concurrent goals to aim for is three. It all but guarantees a player has something to pursue while still being able to focus. As goals are completed, the player should replace them with new ones, either right away (less common) or after an adventure or two gives them something new to think about (more common).

NARRATIVE GOAL DESIGN

Another less mechanical way to frame goals is in terms of character arcs and storytelling. In this framing, completing a long-term goal represents a full character arc, after which that character's story has been told. A good example of this is Frodo's goal of "destroy the One Ring" in the *Lord of the Rings* trilogy. This goal is so difficult to complete and involves so many other adventures (comprising three books!) that Frodo is completely changed by the time he accomplishes it. The act of completing his long-term goal forms the full arc of the character.

A mid-term goal tells a story in which a character learns something or is changed by it. Another example can be found in *The Lord of the Rings*, when Legolas and Gimli learn to rely on each other as allies. Their mid-term goal in *The Two Towers* (find the missing Merry and Pippin) culminates in a lasting change for both of them, but it's not the end of their story.

A short-term goal is more of a means to an end. In storytelling terms, this is a goal a character completes in order to work toward a larger objective. We see an example again in *The Lord of the Rings* when Aragorn summons the Army of the Dead to the Stone of Erech. His short-term goal of "raise an army to march across Gondor" was completed here, but it serves the narrative purpose of propelling him toward the long-term goal of reclaiming his ancestral throne.

2. Goals should have varying time frames.

Encourage your players to think of goals as being short-term, mid-term or long-term. You'll want a variety of time-to-complete lengths because you want players to direct most of their focus on one thing, with occasional detours toward secondary goals. Designing goals to be completed at different times helps prioritize them in a way that feels organic (because it is).

A short-term goal can be completed in just a few play sessions, and the character is usually powerful enough to tackle it right away. A mid-term goal will take some time to complete and may be impossible without gaining power, skills or hard-to-find information. Consider anything that will take more than six play sessions to complete to be a mid-term goal.

Long-term goals are usually what the campaign is about in a grand sense, so completing them should be the primary driver of your campaign. Long-term goals can be as cosmic as "ascend to godhood" or as personal as "learn to love again."

For players looking to abide by our rule and create three goals for their characters, have them think of one mid-term or long-term goal, then one or two short-term goals in service of them.

3. Goals must be achievable.

This might seem straightforward, but it's not. Of course, we want our goals to be achievable—that's why we pursue them! But what "achievable" means in this sense is "measurable." Goals should be formulated in such a way that we know when we have attained them.

Consider the goal, "I want to become more powerful." A fine goal for a martially minded party member, but is it achievable? It depends on how we measure "powerful." A better goal bakes the subjective measurement of power, as determined by the character, into the wording: "I want to win in a real duel against an opponent who is much stronger than me." That goal expresses the same desire ("to be more powerful") but it's much easier to tell when the player is successful. They could also go with the variations of "I want to win the martial arts tournament in Songul next year" or "I want to single-handedly defeat Drathul the Dread-Winged" to add more interesting and more specific plot elements to the goal.

If the Game Master is reading through player goals and can imagine an encounter or reward that, once completed or attained, will clearly indicate the goal has been reached, it is an achievable goal. For example, if a character's goal is to "get revenge on the fallen paladin who killed my mentor," then an encounter in which the character fights and defeats that paladin clearly indicates the goal has been reached. If not, that player should brainstorm some encounters or rewards that might serve this purpose, or perhaps the goal needs to be changed a bit.

4. Goals must have consequences for failure.

When a player's goal is achievable, it must also be possible to fall short of it. Failure changes us. Sometimes we learn from it, other times we just live with the sting of defeat (which will also change us). The idea here is to construct a goal such that any outcome will advance the plot. If the character accomplishes the goal and gets what they wanted, the Game Master and player will reassess, adjust the world and formulate new goals. Ideally, the same process will take place if a character fails a goal. In this case, there will be a penalty for failure, the world will be adjusted and the player will formulate new goals.

The penalty for failure does not always have to be mechanical, like death or losing a character level. In fact, the best penalties are story-related. Did you fail to secure the gate to the city? The invading army rolls in and crushes the neighborhoods closest to the gate. Now you get to deal with the aftermath. Did you fail to uncover the identity of the killer? They strike again, and this time the victim is a friend or loved one.

Don't be afraid to make these penalties personal, since doing so drives the plot forward. You should, however, make sure the consequences of failure are clear. These consequences don't need to be stated as part of the goal or even explicitly decided on beforehand, but players should have a good idea of what they'll face if they fail.

For example, failing to discover the secret last word in a spell might mean it misfires (or worse, backfires). However, failing to convince a human settlement that a horde of gnolls is on the way shouldn't mean that the gnolls automatically wipe out the settlement. Instead, the players should understand that, should they fail in their goal of warning the settlement, the humans will be unprepared for the gnoll attack and the encounters they face will be based on that fact: the fights will be more deadly, the humans will be unorganized, the defenses will be down, etc.

Finally, the character goals a player chooses do not have sufficient consequences for failure if they are repeatable. If you can fail at achieving a goal only to try it again, then it doesn't mean anything to fail. If the only penalty for failing to open the rune-covered door (to achieve the mid-term goal of "find my father's missing arcane dagger") is that you must come try again, it shouldn't have been a player goal—it should have been a skill check. Instead of letting the party try their hand at unlocking the door once again, explain as they arrive that another adventuring group has left their calling card within, indicating that the loot and the dagger are still in play, but now a more difficult obstacle is in place.

5. Goals must be fun to pursue.

This is the hardest rule to explain. After all, fun is subjective, and what is enjoyable for your group might be a drag for another table of players. If you read a player's goal and it seems like it might not be fun to play, don't be afraid to ask them about it and see if you can tweak it.

In general, you can spot goals that are fun to play by seeing if you can think of a few level-appropriate obstacles to throw in the party's way as they pursue the goal. Goals that you can't think of level-appropriate obstacles for (either because they're too easy, too hard or too difficult to dream up) are probably not going to be fun to play. If a 1st-level wizard wants to become a lich, that's a good long-term goal, but it's not going to be fun for a while—they'll need to focus on other things first. Alternatively, if a 20th-level wizard wants to learn a passed-over spell from the early levels, that's an inappropriately easy

MILESTONE LEVELING WITH GOALS

Typically, our games use a milestone leveling system (in which you don't track player experience points but instead award levels after major story beats). We've found that having concrete goals that players work toward makes milestone leveling very easy. The GM simply award levels when goals are attained (sometimes we add a combat experience requirement if the setting calls for it). We can even have players with characters of different levels based on how many of their own personal goals they have attained, or a party of equal levels if we award levels to characters who help others attain their goals. You should do what works for your table.

goal and not very fun to play.

In each case, we can think of ways to make the goal more fun: We can introduce the idea of progressive mastery of necromancy for the 1st-level wizard, and perhaps some mystical restriction or trial for the 20th-level wizard. In each case, we've transformed the goal into something that meets our criteria without actually replacing it.

You might occasionally discover a goal isn't fun during play. When this happens, don't be afraid to find a way to make it more enjoyable, either by rewriting it, introducing a twist or just pretending it never happened. Fun is the point of the game, and goals should never get in the way of that.

It's best (and more fun) to have your players formulate their goals while you're together at the table. This allows players to riff off of each other's ideas and to design goals that complement one another. Just as players may select the mechanics of their characters to work well together (classes, spells, equipment, etc.), players who design goals together can think about how they might cooperate to achieve what their characters want. As the game develops, players can continue to share their goals with the table and collaborate as they pursue them.

PLAYER GOALS IN ACTION

We've been playing with these ideas for a while as we gained experience as Game Masters, and we consider our decision to require these goals as one of the first and most important steps we took toward improving. Here are a few examples of well-designed player goals from games we've run in the past few years.

CASE STUDY #1

"I want to free my hometown from the rule of the orc clans."

One of our 5e players created an elf paladin named Naivara Amakiir, a warden of the great northern forests in the lands where we set our game. She mentioned her forest settlement had been overrun by orcs in her youth, and she had been hunting the responsible tribe through the forests ever since. She chose a short-term goal of freeing her hometown from the rule of the clans. This was a great starting point because it had a clearly identifiable success state (Rule #3).

We suggested she make more of a story out of it and say the orcs had turned her hometown into a fort and a base of operations from which they were attacking other elven settlements in the region. That made the task much harder and turned it into a mid-term goal (Rule #2), since she had to gather support and allies before taking on the fortified orc settlement. Naivara convinced the party to go north to secure the assistance and rewards of her people. They spent levels 6 through 9 adventuring in those forests, culminating in a great battle to reclaim the fort. If she failed, she knew the orc attacks would continue and the retaliation would be brutal (Rule #4).

This is a very traditional fantasy example, but it worked perfectly in our proactive game. Naivara's player didn't just say "my character dislikes orcs" based on her backstory—she made that element of her story a fundamental aspect of her character, and the pursuit of that particular goal (she had others, too—see Rule #1) was her expression of that aspect. The group got a lot of mileage out of it too, since it sent them up north, into more dangerous lands, and the climactic battle was a great way to end that arc of the campaign (Rule #5: have fun!).

"*I want to break the curse plaguing my family line.*"

One of our more creative players made a human wizard named Telomarp, son of Telomerp, son of Telomere, whose family line was cursed with each successive generation being worse than the previous one. The long-term goal of breaking the family curse was fantastic for game prep, since it allowed us to introduce different avenues to explore as short-term goals related to the curse-breaking (see Rule #2). How far was he willing to go to break the curse, we wondered? Would he seek answers from the mages' college? Or turn to the knowledgeable Sapphire Order of the Stormwatcher, a cult that worshiped a blue dragon sorcerer? Would he stoop to making a pact with a demon?

This goal also allowed us to riff off of his ideas. Telomarp often asked important NPCs about lifting curses and then brainstormed with his party members about ways to break the curse. I was able to listen to these ideas, pick out some exciting ones and dangle them in front of him the following session. Whatever he thought was interesting, he pursued (Rule #5).

Telomarp's goal is fairly open-ended, but it is still achievable in the sense of Rule #3. This game is still ongoing, so Telomarp hasn't broken the curse yet, but he is getting closer. Once he manages to do it, we'll throw in a few exciting obstacles for him and the rest of the party to tackle, then we'll have our goal "achieved" by talking about the curse breaking, what that means for the character and new goals to pursue from that point (Rule #1).

CASE STUDY #3

"I want to replace my fleshy body with one of steel and chrome."
In one of our Blades in the Dark games, a player created Azzik, AKA Skitter, an Akorosi Leech (sort of a mad inventor class). Azzik hated the weakness of human flesh and aspired to something greater. After a few adventures in which his body failed him, he created the long-term goal of becoming a techno-magical cyborg.

This goal was a blast to pursue, as Azzik was always experimenting on himself, seeking out powerful (if volatile) material components and trading secrets with dangerous entities in order to achieve perfection. In his pursuit of his goal, which took dozens of sessions and eight real-life months, he established and chased many short- and mid-term goals (Rule #1 and #2), stole a dragon's hoard-worth of materials, experimented on human subjects and nearly died twice (Rule #5).

FURTHER BENEFITS OF THIS EXAMPLE

OK, for the record, I was the player who brought Azzik to life, so I can say firsthand this style of play also felt extremely fun on the player's end. Goal-setting isn't just a benefit to the GM for making encounter design easier—it empowers players to make meaningful choices and therefore have a better time. The campaign was a blast because our decisions really mattered—we felt like movers and shakers without feeling like gods. We wanted to form a gang, we wanted to start a pseudo-revolution, we wanted to rob the most dangerous organization of cultists in the city if only so we could all become machine-men; we came up with all of these ideas as a group, and Jonah designed the encounters around them. The goals we set for ourselves were a massive improvement overall to our agency in the game, especially for a TTRPG so focused on wild plans and ill-advised heists. —*TF*

The best part is that when he finally achieved his goal and became a cyborg, he didn't stop there. His character had learned the hard way, through his pursuit of the goal, of the "weakness of the flesh," and decided his new long-term goal was to "usher in a new age of enlightenment brought by the fusion of all men with machines" (this one strains Rule #3, but his conviction made me think it was achievable).

This is a good example of a goal that emerged organically out of play (in this case, a few botched combat rolls), made sense with the character's backstory and abilities, fit the vibe of the setting and the group and made a good springboard for future play. All of these things made it easy for me to build encounters around it. Azzik's player had a good time thinking up outlandish science experiments to run, and I had a good time thinking up equally outlandish ways they might go wrong (Rule #4).

CASE STUDY #4

"I want to sleep with the diplomat from Iruvia."

In the same Blades game as Azzik, one player created Cobb AKA Footsie, an Iruvian Slide (a playboy con-man character) who wanted to sleep with a certain NPC. I usually roll my eyes at the "I roll to seduce" jokes (I've been playing this game for almost 20 years, so I've heard a lot of them), but this one ended up working extremely well.

The goal made sense for his "foreigner in a strange land"-type character, and his love interest was well-connected with one of the gangs involved in several other players' goals and wanted a few things from the players' crew anyway. It was short-term, setting-appropriate, achievable and would serve as a springboard for other adventures if it was achieved (Rules #3 and #4). To make things interesting, we decided that Cobb would catch feelings for the NPC and would jump through a series of increasingly ridiculous hoops to be with her. This let me put the party through the wringer with political intrigue, espionage and sabotage. These were all things they wanted to do anyway, but with Cobb's goal as a lever, I could connect those interests to a larger story about changing politics in the city.

After the Iruvian diplomat finally fell for Cobb and they got together, a heist gone wrong meant the Iruvian consulate had to distance themselves from the crew of scoundrels, and Cobb and his lover drifted apart. At a crossroads, Cobb's player decided he would have Cobb try to move on by throwing himself into another romance with another woman who turned out to be a demon in disguise. His failure to complete his short-term goal, "get over my breakup by finding a new lover" (Rule #4) threw the crew into even more dangerous adventures. Something that started as a funny way to get Cobb to care about the city he was in ended up being one of the driving forces of our plot. This relatively ribald goal worked for our table, and I knew the players would go for it based on their responses to the "content and boundaries" survey I start each new campaign with, but you should always collaborate with your table about what you're comfortable with in your games.

CASE STUDY #5

"I want to become a famous bard."

We wanted to include a bad example in our case studies too, so we can show what doesn't make for good proactive play. We didn't ask the player to change this goal after they came up with it, and it ended up not being enjoyable to play. It wasn't actively harmful to the game (hopefully you'll catch a goal like that before the game starts!), but we had just started asking players for character goals and didn't know what to look for yet.

There are a few things that make this goal hard to play around. You have probably spotted a few already. The first, and the most obvious, is that it's too vague (not achievable per Rule #3). What does it mean to be famous? We could have improved this by making this goal more specific and tied to certain events, such as, "I want to perform for the royal court" or "I want to write a rude song about the king that gets me thrown in jail" or even "I want to be recognized by a stranger on the street by the sound of my voice alone."

This goal also didn't have meaningful consequences for failure (Rule #4). What would happen if the bard didn't become famous? They would just be sad and keep trying. In order to improve the goal, we needed to decide what failure would look like and how it would affect the world of our game.

These changes, while they would have helped, wouldn't have solved the fundamental problem we ran into: It just didn't fit well with the other characters' goals. The current game was about trudging through plains of ash in a dying world, and the other goals

BACKWARD CHARACTER DESIGN

There is something to be said for the "backward" approach to character design: coming up with fun character goals first, then designing a character around those goals. For example, you could choose the setting-related goal of "usurp the goblin king," then ask yourself: What sort of character might have this goal? What skills and abilities would they have? Who would they know? What would they be like? This is an advanced maneuver: It's a lot of fun but often requires a bit more creative energy than starting with your character design first.

were about reigniting the sun and delving into lost dungeons. There just wasn't much space to accommodate for the "famous bard" angle in the setting or drive of our story. We wanted to inject a little lightheartedness in an otherwise grim setting, so we went for it, but the player ended up not having fun trying to pursue that long-term goal. He came to us with that concern, so we made a few changes.

The player decided to have his cheerful bard seek stories and songs from before the world went dark and play them for people to bring some warmth to their lives. His new goal, "perform the songs from the lost sacred hymnal of the Church of the Sun for the citizens of Torchlight" was concrete, achievable, made sense for the character and went well with all the dungeon-delving the group was already doing. He broke the goal down into a few mid-term goals (finding the hymnal, learning the songs, securing a performance space) and even more short-term goals. The process was simple, since he had a clear long-term goal to divide into steps. Making these changes totally turned his experience around.

APPLYING THIS PRACTICE TO YOUR GAME

You've now read enough player-generated goals to see how crucial they are to proactive fantasy games. If you're ready to implement this practice in your own game, we highly recommend making it a part of character creation, as described in the timeline in the introduction. If you do a Session 0 in which you make new characters, this is the perfect time to discuss character goals. Wait until most of the character is finished first—you'll want class, personality traits and backstory ironed out before you ask players to think about specific goals. Having the other players there allows for more cooperation between goals, more closely aligned goals and more creativity as

PRACTICE EXERCISE

Think about one of your own characters from a game you recently played. If you haven't played in a game, or it's been so long you don't remember, think of a fantasy character from a book you read or a show you watched recently. With this character in mind, try answering the following questions:

1. What is a mid-term goal this character has? Remember, it doesn't need to be world-shattering, but it needs to be important to them and difficult to accomplish.
2. What are one or two short-term goals that would help the character work toward that mid-term goal?
3. Finally, what are two or three obstacles that stand in the way of the character achieving one of those short-term goals? Could any of them be encounters?

Example Answers: I recently played a fighter/rogue/barbarian grappler multiclass (don't ask) named Morn Helstag. When he was young, his sister was kidnapped by the fey and replaced with a changeling, but now, 20 years later, he has seen her in a dream and believes she is still alive.

1. Morn's mid-term goal is "find my kidnapped sister."
2. In order to do that, he'll need to complete the short-term goals of "figure out how she sent me the message in the dream" and "find a portal into the Feywild."

Note: In order to complete the second goal, the GM must make sure Morn (and the party) locate lore about a long-lost Feywild portal, navigate a forbidding wilderness, fight past the portal's guardians and successfully activate it. These encounters are easily defined and flow directly from the stated goals. Notice how Morn's character led him to choose the short-term goals of determining how the dream worked and finding a portal. Morn's character traits are revealed in his framing of his goal, and then further explored in the adventures he goes on as he pursues that goal. If Morn had chosen different short-term goals, the Game Master could have designed totally different encounters to represent obstacles.

players bounce ideas off each other.

As players complete goals and begin establishing new ones (or as characters die and take their list of goals to the grave, making room for a new character to emerge from the ashes), make sure to re-engage with the rules of goal-setting at the table as you go. It's easier to keep everyone on the same page and you'll often get creative input from other players. If you prefer to have players bring pre-made characters to your game, or if someone is bringing an already-established character to a new setting, you should still have clarifying conversations about their goals at the table. A simple "What are your character's goals? What are they after?" and a few detail-seeking follow-up questions should do it (see Chapter 2 for more information on clarifying goals for existing characters).

For those epic, long-term goals, choosing a new course after completion might not be enough. If a character's arc is over and it's time for them to retire, don't be afraid to have them sail off into the West. You can always introduce a new character if you'd like to keep playing or keep the character with the completed story arc around long enough to help the other characters (their best friends by this point, probably) complete their long-term goals.

Once you have your character goals down, the adventures and plotlines will proceed from there. We'll discuss that in more detail in the final chapter, where we put all this stuff together. For now, think about the goals your players or your character might have and some adventure ideas that might flow naturally from them.

A FEW SPECIFIC SUGGESTIONS

If you or your players are having trouble coming up with fun goals to play, or if you want to try the goals-first method of character creation mentioned on pg. 37, here are a few random tables to use. All the character goals generated from these tables should fit the rules of fun outlined earlier in this section, and you should adapt them to your own needs for your own campaign. These work best as jumping-off points for more creativity, not as out-of-the-box solutions.

Roll 1d20 for each column and mash the results together into a sentence to form your new character goal like this: "My character wants to (objective) because of (reason), but (complication)."

1d20	Objective	Reason	Complication
1	Win the heart of a certain person.	A deep-seated desire to be loved.	It's all a big misunderstanding.
2	Discover the true identity of an important person.	A pathological need to be appreciated or admired.	A rival is interested in the same thing.
3	Return to their homeland.	A genuine sense of concern for others.	Doing so would anger a local politician.
4	Slay a powerful monster.	A promise to a dying family member or friend.	It's really, really far.
5	Defend a group or settlement from an impending attack.	Spite, plain and simple.	Someone else has done it already, but they did it wrong.
6	Discover the location of a fabled natural feature.	A hunger for power.	They're unknowingly missing a key piece of information.
7	Destroy a powerful magical artifact.	A quest of self-improvement.	A location involved is very dangerous for this character specifically.
8	Obtain a powerful magical artifact.	The search for spiritual enlightenment.	They have sworn a vow that makes it much harder to do.
9	Find and recover a kidnapped or missing friend or family member.	Everyone else was doing it.	There is a religious prohibition against doing so.

10	Claim an ancestral birthright or fortune.	It just seemed like fun.	An injury prevents them from doing so.
11	Defend or mentor an important young person.	A prophecy they heard and believe says they will.	A person integral to doing so is hostile to them.
12	Prove the existence of a certain phenomenon or being that is thought to be fictional.	A prophecy they have never heard says they will, and fate keeps pulling them toward it.	A persistent misconception means they are mistaken.
13	Forge a peace or alliance between two groups.	The pay was too good to turn down.	Two other groups are involved in the same goal.
14	Conceal a secret by destroying evidence or a person.	Revenge.	The trail has gone cold.
15	Interrupt a ritual or spell that would cause a grand negative effect.	Prove themselves worthy of a love interest who does not return their feelings.	A classic switcheroo has confused similar people or items.
16	Destroy or neutralize a certain powerful person.	Restore their family's good name.	Two factions or people who do not get along must cooperate to make this happen.
17	Reconnect with an important person they used to be close with.	Get the attention of a potential patron.	An important person or object is accidentally destroyed before much progress is made.
18	Discover their own true identity as an important person.	An inexplicable compulsion that's probably related to childhood somehow.	Doing so would break an important treaty.
19	Learn important knowledge that has been concealed or locked away.	Gain experience in a skill needed for another task.	It has literally never been done before.
20	Kill a god.	God told them to.	The god's followers are proficient fighters.

Using Goals in Practice

In the chapters that follow, we'll talk about how to make the goals your players generate the center of your game. We'll discuss how to design your encounters, adapt your NPCs and locations and create fun rewards that all center around the things your players want to accomplish.

That could mean a lot of work if your party's goals are scattered. It's a hassle to run four different games for four different players, which is essentially what you're doing if your four players have four disparate goals. Instead, guide your players during their goal formulation process to ensure that when the smoke clears, everyone's path forward is somewhat related. Players will naturally do this as they collaborate on their goal creation, and you may find that the character who wants to topple a local warlord and the character who wants to avenge their family's death at the hands of a local warlord have a common interest

IS THIS LAZY STORYTELLING?

We've had conversations with other Game Masters who claim that building your game's world around your players' characters in this way is "lazy storytelling." We told those Game Masters, respectfully, that if that was how they felt about running tabletop RPGs, they should go write a novel instead. If the story of your game cannot unfold any other way than the way you've already decided it will go, and if you aren't going to adapt it to the characters that drive it forward, then why are you playing with other people? For us, the joy of getting together for game nights is discovering the story together through co-construction of the fantasy with friends. Adapting your world (or the adventure you bought or downloaded) or even creating it out of whole cloth to suit the characters at the table is the foundation of co-telling. —*JF* that's easily identifiable. Other goals will take more work to connect.

As you listen to your players talk about the goals they'd like to chase, consider which goals you can bundle together. Could the ancient spell the wizard seeks be contained in the same crypt as the old sage the necromancer wants to talk to? Could the keep that the cleric's god wants to claim be located near the goblin cave the fighter wants to clear out for coin? You can connect the objects, locations and NPCs involved in your players' goals in ways that will bind the party together and give them a strong reason to keep adventuring as a unit.

In order to do any of that, though, you'll need to know what your party's goals (long-, mid- and short-term) are at any given time. Make sure you're keeping a running list of the goals each party member has set, accomplished and failed to achieve. As you read through the chapters of this book, you'll see that having quick access to your party's goals means you'll be able to generate appropriate encounters, treasure and NPCs on the fly. Worry about connecting those goals

PLAYER GOAL TRACKING

I keep track of my players' goals on a single sheet of notebook paper at the front of my binder. Each player has about 10 blank lines devoted to them that I fill in with their long- and mid-term goals as the campaign develops. As I'm thinking about encounters to design for the next game session, I can look at all these goals in one place and build my game around them. I write the short-term goals in my notes for the session in which the player states them, since these usually don't persist for longer than a session or two before they're solved. If you're just starting out tracking your party's goals, you might find it more useful to track these short-term goals on the same sheet as the mid- and long-term goals. —*JF* later, when you are actually running the game. For now, just make a note of them to make your life easier later.

While the preceding pages might make it seem like introducing player goals to your game is complicated, it's actually quite simple. Follow the steps below to introduce character goals to your game at any stage.

Player Step: Think about your character's backstory, abilities and character traits. Explain them to the group.

Player Step: Come up with a long- or mid-term goal.

Game Master Step: Is this goal achievable? Does it seem fun? How could it fail forward?

Player Step: If necessary, rework the goal until it meets the criteria.

Player Step: Share goals with the table and adjust to collaborate better if needed.

Game Master Step: Record each player's long-term goal.

Player Step: Create one or two short-term goals that contribute to your long-term goal.

Game Master Step: Is this goal achievable? Does it seem fun? How could it fail forward?

Player Step: If necessary, rework the goal until it meets the criteria.

Player Step: Share goals with the table and adjust to collaborate better if needed.

Game Master Step: Record each player's short-term goal. Think about if any of these goals involve the same places, people or objects and make a note of that, too.

Notice how in the process outlined above, the players are responsible for creating the direction of the game, and the Game Master is responsible for facilitating and organizing the game. That's the key to proactive play, and it's why we've divided the responsibilities so clearly. A group of players who decide what will be fun and then goes and does it will have fun. It's as simple as that.

In the chapters that follow, you'll consult the goals created by this checklist over and over again, so make sure they're in an easy-to-reach spot. It's time to get to the behind-the-scenes work of making a proactive game run smoothly.

Player Steps	Game Master Steps
Think about this character's backstory, abilities and traits. Explain them to the group. Come up with a long- or mid-term goal.	Is this goal achievable? Does it seem fun? How could it fail forward?
If necessary, rework the goal until it meets the criteria. Share goals with the table and adjust to collaborate better if needed.	Record each player's long-term goal.
Create one or two short-term goals that contribute to your long-term goal.	Are these goals achievable? Does it seem fun? How could it fail forward?
If necessary, rework the goal until it meets the criteria. Share goals with the table and adjust to collaborate better if needed.	Record each player's short-term goals. Think about if any of these goals involve the same places, people or objects and make a note of that, too.

Chapter 2

—•—ε·ʒ—•—

FACTIONS

R UNNING AN ENGAGING tabletop game is all about encouraging your players to be proactive, take risks and change the face of the world. It's important to balance this element of the game with a healthy dose of circumstances they can't control or else the game becomes about characters as powerful as gods playing in a sandbox that only they can affect, which is hardly challenging, even if it is a bit of fun.

The way we balance this equation is with opposition: Across the table from your heroes are the "factions" of the fantasy world, the organizations and groups that change the world alongside, and often in opposition to, the players. These factions and their members have their own goals and pursue them concurrently with the players. It's the push and pull of action between the player goals and faction goals that create a living world and an exciting experience at the table.

According to the philosophy of proactive fantasy, the players should guide the action. Therefore, the players should act first and set the events of your adventure or campaign in motion. But once that ball is rolling, the factions you create should sweep into the space the players have created and pursue their own goals relentlessly at the expense of the players and each other. For this reason, it is useful to think of factions, not individual NPCs, as the GM-controlled counterparts of the party.

Designing Factions

A faction is a group of people organized around shared interests. In classic fantasy, what we call factions take many forms: adventurer's guilds, town councils, wizarding schools, etc. With prior knowledge of the faction's makeup and some easy assumptions about its interests based on members' actions (the local village council comprises elders who want to stop the recent disappearances of townspeople in the surrounding woods), your players will know all they need to in order to plan around

BORROWING FACTION IDENTITY FROM CHARACTER BACKSTORIES

If you collect backstories from your players ahead of time, you can use them to flesh out factions to populate your world and ensure your early plot hooks are directly tied to PC goals. You can also glean some information about character traits and histories to help you decide how the factions you might already have in mind will interact with the party. For example, if a player mentions they learned their cleric spells when they served in the Moonghosts, a secret werebeast-hunting organization, you might replace one of your planned religious factions with the Moonghosts instead, filling in some important details using information from the PC's past. That information might also change your plans for the party's interactions with a local government with a prominent werebeast member: Will the Moonghosts get involved? Will the character's past interfere with their judgment of the situation? What are some ways you can increase or decrease the tension in that relationship by involving elements of the hunter character's backstory? —JF and with the faction (they might offer to find the missing townsfolk or connect the disappearances to another goal they're pursuing) and you can improvise more details and backstory later as necessary.

If you have a game idea in mind, or if you're adapting an existing adventure for proactive play, you likely already know the factions you'll need to flesh out. For each faction, consider the way it interacts with the world and where its aims might overlap with your players'. This will allow you to orchestrate a plot point tug-of-war. To create and introduce a faction, first outline some goals by determining the following (Note: if you're adapting a published adventure, use any given background information—and your imagination—to decide these):

Faction Identity

What is the faction and what does it do? Start with a brief idea of the role the faction plays in your world. Feel free to use shortcuts like archetypes (pg. 53), existing ideas and even character backstories as inspiration to get a rough idea of what this organization is all about. Let the rule of cool prevail here—decide on a faction identity based on aesthetics and the role you need them to play within your game, either as antagonists, allies or something in between.

Area of Operation

Decide where this faction is most active and areas into which they might want to expand. The location of the faction can give you a clearer idea of its existing goals and possible conflicts.

Power Level

Decide how powerful this faction is. What are the resources at its disposal? If conflict—armed or otherwise—arises, how likely is it this faction will come out on top? This information will help you determine when factions act and when they choose to sit out.

IDEOLOGY

Finally, you'll need to establish a few core principles of your faction's ideology. Why do they do what they do? What do they believe about their role in the world? This is the most important step and will help you decide how they act when you design short-, mid- and long-term goals for your faction.

If you establish the Faction Identity, Area of Operation, Power Level and Ideology in order, you'll have a clear idea of who your faction is, what they want and how they will pursue their goals. This is usually enough to improvise goals later on when they become relevant, but you might choose to generate a few when you first design the faction to get you started. For an example of these steps in action, see the example adventure planning process in Chapter 8.

Create your factions with this principle in mind: Dramatic tension arises when two people or organizations have goals that are in conflict. The next few sections of this chapter will guide you through using the faction identity you have created to design long-term faction goals. We'll leave the mid- and short-term goals mostly to the NPCs that represent the factions. See Chapter 3 for more on how to flesh out your factions with NPCs.

As you outline your faction's goals, make sure they overlap with your party's goals to ensure the two will collide. Include a healthy mix of closely aligned, somewhat aligned and conflicting goals to make your world feel dynamic and alive. There will be factions that are interested in things entirely unrelated to the PCs and their goals, but those merely add color rather than thematic relevance to your game (unless of course your players decide otherwise). To put a spotlight on the action and the PCs, make sure your factions have goals that relate to the same people, places and events as your PCs' goals. This ensures that as the players and factions pursue their goals independently, unexpected and exciting changes will sweep across your game world.

Common Faction Archetypes

GOVERNMENT

In this context, "government" refers to any faction that exerts authority over a group of people or a territory through community organization, the promise of protection from outside enemies and the threat of punishment from within the authority apparatus. A traditional feudal aristocracy can be a government, as can a democratically elected senate. But a rag-tag group of freedom fighters can also form a government in a lawless land if they do things like mete out justice and provide security from roving bandits. Even something like a deep-thinking AI can be a government if it performs the functions outlined above.

We want to make this distinction between governments and other factions because of the role governments play in classic fantasy games, which will inform our understanding of what governments should do in our proactive fantasy games.

GOVERNMENT GOALS

In most classic fantasy, the government is a force of stability and order. Its priorities are to preserve itself as an organization (though not necessarily the people within it) and to keep the peace (which is relative). This places the government in a boring but very useful position in the context of our game. We can safely assume the government of a region will support goals and movements that preserve the status quo and will oppose (often with violence) those goals and movements that disrupt existing order in the region.

These tendencies exist at every level of government. A classic example to consider from Robert Jordan's *The Wheel of Time* series is the local government organizations in the rural town of Emond's Field in the Two Rivers, far from the influence of the Andoran crown. Two factions, the Town Council and the Women's Circle, exist to preserve the social and economic order in Emond's Field. They do so by organizing town events, resolving disputes and supporting trade. They don't do this passively, either. They have active goals that are smaller-scale versions of these same "higher" principles: hiring a gleeman for Bel Tine, bringing Wit Congar before the council to plead his case (even against his will!) and making sure the peddler Padan Fain comes by at the right time of year, just to name a few.

Now consider the court of Queen Morgase of Andor, who rules over thousands of square miles of heartland (including the Two Rivers from the above example). The Crown values the same things as our local government, and its goals also revolve around preserving social and economic order. Because it has more territory, the Crown must consider more goals than the government of Emond's Field does: Instead of organizing town events, the Crown must gather taxes from the whole region; instead of resolving local disputes, the Crown must keep Andor out of war (or win existing wars); instead of supporting trade in the town, the Crown must consider exports and imports and the assets and debts of the entire region. The specific shape these goals take will therefore be different: recruit a brave tax collector to send to the pesky Two Rivers, host a diplomatic meeting to defuse border disputes with Cairhien, find a way to import grain to supplement a dry year's crop, etc.

Cyllic-5 Local Council

In a space opera fantasy game I ran recently, the players landed on a frontier planet known for its heavy metal gaseous seas. The local government there, a branch of the galactic empire in our setting, was made up of citizens who were locally elected to represent their planet. Though they technically presided over the whole planet, much of it was inaccessible to humans without special equipment, so their reach was limited to the rocky continents and shallow seas on one side of the planet . Given the planet's distance from the galactic core and the importance of the heavy metal trade, the local government enjoyed a great deal of autonomy and power, and they had the resources to deal with most on-planet problems, though they wouldn't stand a chance against the Empire itself. For my game, I wanted a *Firefly*-esque tone of hardscrabble people on the frontier doing the best with what they had, so I decided to make my local council fiercely independent, distrustful of outsiders and willing to use violence to preserve the rights and privileges of their citizenry.

The last element of the Cyllic-5 Local Council I needed to determine was its immediate goals. Since the players didn't interact with the government at all in the first session, I was able to hold off on this decision. In the aftermath of the first session, though, a religious cult claimed autonomous control over a small territory on the shores of the gaseous sea, threatening heavy metal extraction there. This was a good reason for the local government to get involved, so I generated a simple mid-term goal for them: "Preserve heavy metal extraction infrastructure at Tencity beach." This put them at odds with the cult, who had a mid-term goal in direct opposition to this: "Expropriate heavy metal extraction infrastructure at Tencity beach." More importantly, it put them on a collision course with the players, who had a short-term goal of "infiltrate the heavy metal extraction infrastructure at Tencity beach and rescue captives there."

Given the Power Level and Ideology of my local government, I decided to formulate these specific short-term goals for the Cyllic-5 Local Council: "Reinforce the armed security around the extractors" and "send the local police to investigate the cult leader and bring him in on any charge." The players, whose short-term goal put them in conflict with government agents trying to carry out their own short-term goals, were thrown into a turf war that turned violent quite quickly, which matched well with the identity/ideology of the factions and the tone of the game. —JF

GOVERNMENT FACTIONS IN PROACTIVE FANTASY

Just like the main characters in the above example collided with the goals of their local governments, we can create interesting government factions in our game to fill out the world and provide more goals that ensure conflict and confrontation with the players. We just have to make sure our government's goals are connected to PC goals.

Notice that at each level of government in the given examples—and all the levels in between—the fundamental goals of the rulers were the same: to preserve order and stability. The methods at their disposal were different, and the specifics of the actions they wanted to take were different as a result, but the principles guiding those actions were very similar. Consider what your PC goals have to do with order and stability in the region that the government faction controls. Would the government respond favorably or unfavorably to those pursuits? How does that response take shape?

When designing government factions, always consider how you can design goals that involve them in the lives of the PCs. If you can't think of any, consult the table or simply introduce the government faction at another time. You can read the PC Goals column opposite to find a goal that matches or is similar to one in your game, then read the Government Faction Goals column in the same row for an idea of how to design the faction goal to overlap with the PC goal, making tweaks as necessary.

For example, if one PC has a mid-term goal of "exact vengeance on a bandit leader who killed my family," we have several choices for a great order-related goal for our government faction. We could have the government take the short-term goal of "eliminate banditry on the roads outside the capital" if we want the PCs and the government to pursue the same goal, or the short-term goal of "collect monthly

PC Goals	Government Faction Goals
Hunt a powerful monster, profit from trade, defend a settlement.	Increase the safety of local roads and trade routes.
Start a peasant revolt, overthrow a corrupt ruler, participate in labor organization.	Suppress an anti-government sentiment among the lower class.
Fight in a certain war, avoid conscription, take a territory.	Raise soldiers for a local army or militia.
Provide war or disaster relief, cause a war or a disaster, profit from a war or disaster.	Organize local factions for war or disaster relief efforts.
Win a dispute against a person, profit from a legal dispute, provide security or military force to someone in a legal dispute.	Settle a legal or social dispute between two parties.
Provide relief to the needy, profit from market manipulation, profit from the sale of items found adventuring.	Address an economic crisis.
Access restricted areas, collect information on an important person, gain admittance to a certain government faction.	Establish a favorable diplomatic relationship with another government faction.
An activity prohibited by a new law was allowed under a old law. Profit from bounty-hunting those who violate the new law.	Enforce a new law.
Install a certain person as ruler, defend the current ruler or governing body, seek independence from a government.	Consolidate power under the current ruler or governing body.
Profit from the trade of a certain region or goods, defend a certain shipment or trade route, gain admittance to a certain trade or government faction.	Secure a favorable trade deal with another government faction.

bribes from the bandit leader" if we want a goal that puts the PCs and the government at odds. If we have a PC with a long-term goal of "claim my ancestral throne," the government faction needs a goal of "eliminate all pretenders to the crown" or "seek out the rightful heir and restore them to the throne." Whatever choice you make should be influenced by how you want the faction to interact with the players and the tone of your game.

LABOR

Labor organizations include guilds, unions, cartels and any other organization that represents the interests of workers. A group of merchants that organizes to ensure fair prices and honest measures, a guild of adventurers that organizes around pooling dungeon loot and a union of ghostly railway workers that organizes around hazard pay are all examples of labor organizations. Compared to government factions, labor organizations are usually weaker and less organized, though exceptions exist. Examples of factions in traditional fantasy settings are myriad and run the gamut from power-mad reactionary organizations with the power of emperors—like *Star Wars's* Trade Federation or the Spacing Guild of Frank Herbert's *Dune*—to the to the largely benevolent and anti-authoritarian and even revolutionary , like Ricard Tumblar and the Noble Warriors of Labor in Brian McClellan's *Powder Mage* trilogy.

Labor factions tend to focus on improving the lives of members. So, generally speaking, the more exclusive a guild, the fewer people benefit from its works and resources and, more importantly, the fewer people have a stake in the guild's agenda. For example, a craftsman's guild probably wants to make materials easier to obtain, which makes their jobs easier but also provides a surplus for the people; a traveling merchant organization probably wants safer roads, which also benefit local folks as they take their goods—or themselves—into town. A guild comprised of bankers or soldiers of fortune, on the other hand, might seek to hoard wealth or instigate conflict in order to fill their own coffers, leaving everyday working people to deal with the considerable fallout. Think of the pyromancers from George R.R. Martin's *A Song of Ice and Fire*: caretakers of a vast store of the deadly chemical weapon known as wildfire, they jealously guard the recipe while encouraging the rulers in the Red Keep to wield its awesome power, giving the pyromancers a unique hold on power in Westeros.

The strength of these organizations comes from the size of their memberships as well as the effectiveness of their various leadership structures. Since nearly everybody works, almost everybody has some connection with a labor or trade faction, and many likely have an affiliation with more than one. Many of the NPCs your party meets may even be members of these types of factions—understanding the pervasive influence of labor and trade in all walks of life can help you as a GM create more rounded NPCs—ones your party will have a stronger reaction to than the stock characters they might be used to.

This makes labor factions a great source of cooperation and conflict with your PCs. These factions are interested in anything that affects the working lives of their many members, so many of the situations the PCs get entangled in will affect these factions in some way. Did the party accidentally cause a cave-in? Laborers will be hired to clear out the mine, and miners will be anxious to get back to work. Did they warn the village of an incoming orc horde? Carpenters, masons, thatchers and other tradesmen will be needed to build the town defenses. What if the party brings a chest full of ancient coins minted in a rare metal to the capital city? Commerce guilds are going to panic about commodity price fluctuation. The ubiquity of these factions allows us to link them to player goals in many creative ways. Use them to your advantage.

LABOR GOALS

Consider the main characters that form the crew of thieves central to Brandon Sanderson's *Mistborn* trilogy. Each of these characters is affiliated with one or more labor organizations from their past, and they leverage these connections in pursuit of their own goals. The carpenters provide cover in their workshops, the traders facilitate smuggling on their barges and the chemists provide the rare metals the crew needs to use their powers. Because labor factions are so intimately involved with the day-to-day running of the world, they make logical partners for Sanderson's main characters as they pursue their lofty goals.

The Faction Identity, Area of Operation, Power Level and Ideology are clearly defined. They are unions of laborers and artisans of different skills (identity) who operate in the poorer parts of the city and some of the outlying rural areas (area). They are under the thumb of the government and fear its military might (power level) and who have a strong interest in a revolutionary change in government (ideology). Their goals are not exactly aligned with the party's goals, but they are close enough that they are willing to provide aid to the party as they pursue their own ends.

LABOR FACTIONS IN PROACTIVE FANTASY

We can create interesting labor factions by imagining the types of people that belong to the organization and what they want, then focusing only on the goals that could involve our PCs. These diverse organizations are large enough that they are filled with many different types of people with many different goals, but we don't need to keep track of them all. We only need to keep track of the goals that the members of the organization share and will organize to pursue: goals that will improve their everyday lives (e.g., favorable trade deals, better working conditions, rights to a certain worksite, securing a contract). Once we have a clear idea of those goals, we can start to narrow them down to the ones we'll feature in our game.

In order to weave these factions into the rest of our plan for the table, we'll need to figure out which PC goals will intersect with which faction's goals, then design faction goals that will engineer interesting opportunities for cooperation or conflict between the party and the faction. Don't underestimate how many of these factions your PC goals will end up interacting with—nearly everything the party does will affect working people in some way.

Given how prevalent they can be, labor organizations run the risk of dominating the faction aspect of your game. Other factions like those from the military or aristocratic realms take their membership from only a select few, but trade guilds involve the majority of a given municipality's population. Though the trade factions might not succeed in their pursuit of goals that pit them against governments and religious factions, the sheer number and influence of labor and trade means they will likely become major players through the quantity (if not quality) of their encounters with your party. Out of all the types we present here (except perhaps criminal organizations, depending on the game), the goals of these factions are also most likely to align with the party's goals—PCs generally have to work for a living too, after all. Though their work as adventurers is unusual, what makes life easier for merchants and craftsmen often makes life easier for adventurers as well.

For this reason, you may wish to limit the influence and power of labor organizations to fit the tone of your setting and culture of your game. In a medieval fantasy setting, the labor factions are usually reduced to a few large guilds, and the political landscape is dominated by governments and religious organizations. In gritty or grim fantasy settings, labor factions are usually controlled or heavily influenced by criminal organizations instead. Find a balance that works for your setting, but be aware that the factions your players choose to support will often come out on top. A little solidarity might change the course of your game.

Once you have a clear idea of how these faction and PC goals interact, you can design encounters around those interactions. These are just as likely to be combat encounters as social or skill encounters. Factions should be willing to fight and bleed for their goals, so don't be afraid to turn up the tension. If you're having trouble thinking of appropriate goals for your labor factions, consider rolling on the table opposite.

To use the table, reference the PC Goals column to find a goal that matches one in your game, then reference the Labor Faction Goals column in the same row for an idea of how to design the faction goal to overlap with the PC goal. These might not fit exactly at first, but by tweaking your faction and negotiating with your players, you can create strong involvement from both parties regardless of the context of the goal itself.

PC Goals	Labor Faction Goals
Get a large architectural project built, help move supplies, help or hurt a criminal organization.	Secure a work contract from a more powerful faction (government/criminal).
Defend a worksite, investigate a dangerous location, suppress a popular movement.	Secure better working conditions (less dangerous/more job protections).
Gain access to a restricted social circle, repay a favor to someone wealthy, exploit a relationship for profit.	Negotiate a trade deal to help members profit.
Obtain a certain item or rare resource, sell an unusual object, find rare reagents or ingredients for a ritual or spell.	Gain a monopoly on a certain item or rare resource.
Impoverish a wealthy person or organization, acquire wealth-producing property, reduce corruption.	Manipulate the market for a certain commodity.
Seek revenge, install an ally in a position of power, take over a faction.	Overthrow or replace its own leadership.
Build a coalition of factions, eliminate competition, mobilize large numbers for a cause.	Ally with, absorb or destroy a related faction.
Gain access to a restricted area, secure the help of a faction leader, undermine a government faction.	Overturn or pass a law to benefit the faction.
Spread religious values, obtain information from locals, profit from a crisis situation.	Directly aid its own members in a crisis situation.
Infiltrate an enemy organization, gain access to a restricted region, find a buyer for illicit goods.	Establish a trade partnership with a known enemy of other powerful factions.

The Rail Jacks

In Blades in the Dark, one of the labor organizations is the Rail Jacks, a group of somewhat-sane individuals who maintain the rails and trains that travel the deathlands outside the city (Identity). The Rail Jacks are distrusted by many citizens and mostly operate outside the city, though the railyard by the city's lightning gates is their undisputed domain (Area). There are only a few hundred Rail Jacks, and while they don't have weapons, they do know a great deal about the trains and find it very easy to load things on or off them without anyone knowing (Power Level). They perform a dangerous and vital job, but the Rail Jacks are distrusted by most of polite society, so alongside their perpetual quest for safer working conditions (Ideology) they are usually seeking approval and acceptance too.

In one of my Blades games, the players wanted to bring down the government but were not nearly powerful enough to even attempt it. Through clever politicking with local factions, including the Rail Jacks, they made a valiant effort. They knew the Rail Jacks were close to striking over a government-imposed change to cargo inspection rules that the Rail Jacks thought was unsafe. The group also knew that without Rail Jacks to process imports and exports, there wouldn't be enough food to go around nor would armed reinforcements be able to swiftly travel from the capital. Because the short-term goals of the two groups ("leverage a strike to get the inspection rules overturned" for the Rail Jacks and "prevent armed reinforcements from entering the city" for the PCs) were perfectly aligned, the players were able to convince the Rail Jacks to strike at exactly the right time to ensure their plan's success.

I didn't design the Rail Jacks faction (it's baked into the Blades setting). But I was able to use the information provided about their Identity, Area, Power Level and Ideology to craft specific goals that benefited the members of the faction and intersected with the PCs' goals in several ways. The players were aware of the faction and knew exactly who to turn to when they needed to shut down travel in and out of the city. —JF

CRIME

A setting's criminal element is usually thought of as a relatively straightforward faction, but that doesn't mean it can't be entertaining. For the purposes of this section, a criminal faction essentially refers to organized crime. A mighty necromancer in a far-off tower is technically a criminal, but that sort of "faction" isn't going to be interacting much with others in the city (except perhaps for increasingly common trips to the morgue followed by a tide of undead spilling into downtown). Additionally, a petty thief (of which the city may have plenty) is not necessarily going to find themselves in the thieves' guild. Because of this, "criminal organization" refers to a network of individuals participating in illegal business and trade. They are usually in direct opposition to the government faction, which wants to enforce law and order. The theme that defines your criminal faction serves a far better purpose than the specific description of its members or exploits.

Overall, criminal factions will differ based on location, setting and a variety of other variables, but the group is likely somewhat organized, must keep their activities hidden from the general public and has a leader (or group of them). Examples of criminal organizations in fantasy include the crew of thieves in the *Mistborn* trilogy the Thieves Guild of *Skyrim* and the Brotherhood Without Banners of *A Song of Ice and Fire*.

CRIMINAL GOALS

A criminal faction's goals usually boil down to "accrue wealth and power" or some variation on that theme, which can be a little stale on its own. What makes a criminal enterprise interesting is not what they're doing (crimes, naturally) but how they pull it off. When developing a criminal faction, consider the how as an extension of the faction's personality in order to add an extra element of intrigue to the mix. A specific criminal goal that overlaps with PC goals, depending on the type of crime, is relatively simple to achieve. Perhaps they're trying to steal something the players want or have or kill someone the players care about (or simply need to keep around awhile). Maybe they burn down the players' favorite tavern after its owner refuses to pay protection money. Crimes generally have victims, and if you put something or someone the players want, like or need in that position, it gives the party the opportunity to pursue or otherwise engage with your criminals. Additionally, criminal organizations need to save face—an embarrassment or insult won't go unpunished, a wrinkle that

PC Goals	Criminal Faction Goals
Source a rare ingredient or expert from a certain part of town.	Start a new protection racket in that part of town.
Obtain a rare crafting material for a personal project or a patron.	Rob a caravan transporting rare crafting materials.
Help a politician outmaneuver rivals.	Blackmail a politician for cash and favors.
Locate a dangerous arms dealer.	Secure a favorable deal with a black market supplier.
Destroy or weaken a criminal faction.	Get revenge on that criminal faction for an insult or violent incident.
Procure a fine steed.	Smuggle a dangerous beast into a city.
Discover the perpetrator of a crime and bring them to justice.	Pay off law enforcement to ignore that crime.
Borrow a precious item from a well-protected vault.	Burgle a famously well-protected vault.
Obtain a powerful magical artifact.	Pass off a forgery as legitimate.
Obtain an antique item from a collector at an auction.	Steal from an auction while all the valuables are under one roof.

CASE STUDY

The Dalthriax Network

In one of my games, a player had written "performing odd jobs for a criminal network" as part of his backstory. His character, a rogue, would occasionally go back to this faction for aid, advice, jobs, allies and a variety of other favors. The faction I created for his character was the Dalthriax Network, a powerful group of criminals that managed most organized crime in the city. The primary goal was typical of such a faction: gain wealth—all their other goals were short-term and pointed to this ultimate aim. But the leader had his own plans, trying to install himself as the city's ruler. The influence this had on the players let me set up the player's goals in opposition to theirs, even though they had allied themselves to the faction. Eventually, this led them to choose between their ideals, and (to my great surprise) they chose the guild, helping the doppelganger leader take control of the city. They did eventually stab him in the back to seize power, but for a time, the allure of the faction's goals outweighed their hatred of the leader. —*TF*

can add interesting epilogues to your adventures.

Goals should exist to further the organization as a whole from a story perspective, but there needs to be some overlap with the players if this faction is to have any bearing on the plot. Allowing a small piece of a criminal faction's goals to overlap with the players' can lead to new encounters—should the party choose to pursue them. Perhaps the players chase after the thieves in a warehouse, or maybe they decide it isn't worth the trouble. The important thing is to let that opportunity arise and let the players decide how to act from there. Player proactivity is key here—when players choose to pursue the faction, this is when encounters begin to arise, even if just by pursuing similar objectives.

If you're having trouble connecting faction goals with criminal goals, refer to the table opposite for inspiration. Just read the PC Goal column to find a goal that best matches one in your game, then read the Criminal Faction Goals column in the same row for an idea of how to design the faction goal to overlap with the PC goal.

RELIGION

Religious sects are an underused subset of factions, but they can be one of the most rewarding, serving as excellent adversaries and/ or allies. Religious groups will, by nature, follow a deity or faith of some kind, and because of this, their goals can be extremely flexible, unusual and fun. Players with religious characters can join these organizations and players with opposing viewpoints can seek to stymie them. Because most religions are ancient (or at least tied to an entity worthy of worship), they often have access to or information regarding powerful tomes, lost relics and magic items. The versatility of religious factions is another welcome boon— because of the variety of gods and pantheons, their priorities and their preferred methods of interacting with the world, religious factions can play any needed role, be it friend, foe or otherwise. Examples of religious factions include the Jedi Council, the Children of the Light and the Knights Radiant of Roshar.

RELIGIOUS GOALS

Religious goals are perhaps the most varied of any faction. Inevitably, a religious faction will follow the desires of their god (who in fantasy is usually a literal god with goals they wish to enact on the Material Plane). One religion may seek to stop violence and heal the sick, while another may wish to sacrifice the purest of heart to bring a thousand years of darkness into the world—dealer's choice.

Religious goals can also be extremely personal: a family member can be brainwashed into a cult, or a kindly old priest may be the father figure of a player. These connections follow the same rules as everything else in proactive fantasy theory—the players need to act in order for factions to react. In a truly proactive game, factions

Serves a God of...	Religious Faction Goals
Health, wellness.	Provide aid, shelter, food and medicine to the poor and sickly.
Power, war.	Support the local army, convert soldiers, infuse weapons with holy energy.
Love, loyalty.	Officiate marriages, promote loyalty, punish betrayers.
Knowledge, intellect.	Acquire rare tomes for the cathedral's library, fund local schools.
Vengeance, justice.	Punish the wicked, make public examples of criminals, root out sources of corruption.
Depravity, hatred.	Find sacrifices for gods, summon demons, slaughter local opposing religious members.
Beauty, perfection.	Support local painters and artists, imbue the area with a holy spell, create the perfect artifact with rare ingredients.
Travel, trade.	Send priests safely on pilgrimages, support local allied trading guilds, acquire accurate maps.

will also pursue their own goals, and encounters are created when their interests and actions overlap with those of the party. If you aren't sure what goal your religious faction would be pursuing, start with the type of god they worship and reference the table above for inspiration.

Overlapping goals are, again, an excellent way to create friction. As with player goals, specificity is our friend. "Summon our dark god to wreak havoc" is very cool but has no substance to stand on. "Burn the Cathedral of Hope to ashes," "Slay the Good Priest Beiros" and "Sacrifice Boblin, Chosen of the Sun God on our altar" could collectively lead to that goal, but there's still more to mine.

Is the Cathedral the player's former home? Is the Good Priest Beiros someone's close friend? And perhaps Boblin, Chosen of the Sun God is a dear ally? A religious faction need not be a cult to be antagonistic to the players. Religious wars, inquisitions, corruption and overly zealous crusaders can all pursue goals that conflict with what the party hopes to achieve. Less aggressive religious factions operate in a similar way, though are often played as far less active. "Obtain the Ring of Heavenly Light," can potentially overlap with players, assuming the party wants to help.

If you're having trouble coming up with religious faction goals that overlap with PC goals, refer to the table opposite.

To demonstrate how widely religious goals can vary, let's look at two examples from fantasy: the Jedi Council from *Star Wars* and the Children of the Light from *The Wheel of Time*.

The Jedi Council is a caste of warrior-priests who advise the highest levels of government. Although their stated and original goals are different, by *Revenge of the Sith*, their primary goal is to preserve their decaying influence. They also have goals related to rooting out the Sith, maintaining control over the child of prophecy and winning the war against the separatist planets. The Jedi have come to believe they are the only ones capable of maintaining this balance.

On the other hand, the Children of the Light are fanatics. They rove the land in armies, killing Aes Sedai and torturing those they believe are Darkfriends. Their goals are opposite to the Jedi—to tear down the established order.

PC Goals	Religious Faction Goals
Receive magical healing.	Reclaim a healing spring site from a band of vile demons.
Help wage a war against an enemy faction.	Enchant the weapons of war-bound crusaders with a holy oil that is in short supply.
Gain the trust of a local noble or well-liked public figure.	Lift a curse on a local noble or well-liked public figure.
Destroy the reputation of a religious faction.	Conceal the knowledge of their faction's past heretical behavior.
Find a buyer for an identified artifact from the ruins of a temple.	Locate the relic of a saint.
Destroy the reputation of a local noble.	Publicly prove that a local noble is a heretic.
Find a missing family member.	Obtain sacrifices for an upcoming blood ritual.
Locate a missing artist.	Commission a work of art or iconography from a well-known artist.
Make a pilgrimage to a holy site in dangerous territory.	Set up a way station to support pilgrims in dangerous territory.
Sway a local government figure to a certain faction's way of thinking.	Convert a local government figure to their religious views.

Tracking Your Factions

How many factions should you include in your game? How closely should you track their goals, assets, key figures and progress?

The right answer to these questions will depend on the culture of your game and your players. In our games, we prefer to actively track no more than a dozen factions, though we may mention a few more to flesh out some aspects of the world. No more than four factions are usually involved with one plot point or important figure, and usually no more than six factions will be involved in a single location, even a large city. You'll notice these familiar numbers—they're to keep factions contained to numbered lists of lengths equal to the number of sides on our favorite dice. If a random faction is needed, or we want to surprise ourselves with a new addition, we can roll randomly to determine a variety of factors.

GOING FROM GENERAL TO SPECIFIC

Now that you have a clear idea of how to design factions guaranteed to create dramatic tension for the players, it's time to get specific. The players won't be interacting with your factions by talking to or fighting with the entire organization at once. Instead, they'll be interacting with specific individuals who represent that faction to the party: NPCs. In the next chapter, we'll discuss how to design these NPCs to encourage proactive play.

Faction Tracking Made Simple

I track this information and keep these notes for one simple reason: consistency. Proactive fantasy games are about the collision of PC goals with the rest of the world. If I forget that the PCs thwarted a certain necromancer's evil ritual, I won't be able to create faction goals that react to the PC goals in a satisfying way. Keeping track of factions, their goals and accomplishments helps keep me honest.

We recommend a simple faction tracking system. For each new faction, record the name, its relative power, the location of its central operations and a brief description. From these elements, immediately create one or two long-term goals (you can refer to the tables in this chapter for ideas). The whole thing takes up about five lines on a piece of notebook paper.

The most important part of faction tracking is keeping a record of progress toward their goals. You can do this with "clocks," a useful story element tracking mechanic from *Blades in the Dark* that we hacked it into all of our games. Here's how it works: A clock is a circle drawn in the margins, divided into four, six, eight or more segments based on how difficult the goal is. As time passes, fill in segments. When it is full, the goal is complete.

You should fill in the clocks for your faction goals based on the PCs' interactions with that faction. Lets take the example of a group of adventurers encountering a *Wicker Man*-style sacrifice about to take place. If the players decide to bring the town council a sacrifice, you might fill the whole clock right away. If they instead bring some local bandits to justice and lock them in the town dungeon, you might fill the clock a little bit to represent a certain unscrupulous town councilman's insistence that the bandits would make good sacrifices. If the players are actively working to prevent the sacrifice, don't fill any segments. The important part is that it's not planned out beforehand—you don't need a list of which actions will fill segments and which don't. Just pay attention to the PCs' actions and do your best to interpret how they affect the goals of the factions you're tracking.—*JF*

Chapter 3

—◦•⚬•‿•⚬•◦—

Non-Player Characters

WHILE FACTIONS ARE the true Game Master-controlled counterpart to the party, players will interact with specific characters from those factions more often than they do the factions as a whole. Think of non-player characters as the face of a faction to which they belong. For factions that feature prominently in your game, there may be numerous "faces"—multiple NPCs with slightly different goals and approaches that all interact with the players differently. In a proactive game, we use these NPCs, their personal goals and the goals they've inherited from their faction to create dramatic tension with the players' goals and make our game exciting.

In this chapter, we'll talk about creating NPCs and defining their goals in relation to the party's. Once we have those goals, we'll talk about what happens when the two are in conflict (Chapter 5, pg. 140). While the world you create can be as diverse and complex as you choose to make it, for the sake of simplicity, faction-fronting NPCs can generally be created so they fit neatly into one of three categories:

1. Allies

NPCs whose goals align with the players' goals.

2. Villains

NPCs whose goals conflict with the players' goals.

3. Patrons

NPCs who grant the players access to the resources of a faction if the party helps advance the patron's and/or the faction's goals.

Each of these NPC archetypes will influence the way your players approach their goals each session. Additionally, these categories are

UNDERSTANDING UNDERLINGS

It's too complicated to track the goals and attitudes of every single NPC in your game. Instead, you should focus on tracking the goals of the faction that your NPCs belong to, except for certain important NPCs. This chapter focuses on the main characters your party will encounter in ways that are directly connected to their own goals, or whose own goals and the pursuit thereof will actually affect the party in some way. It doesn't matter much to the party if the barfly sitting next to them at the tavern dreams of being a great bard one day until the party decides that's important, so you don't plan for that ahead of time. You can assume most NPCs who aren't vital to the plot align with the faction they belong to. This includes the random people your party will meet on the street, the faceless monsters they will fight in a villain's lair, even their own hired underlings. These characters serve to stand in for the goals of their organizations instead of representing themselves. Your players will do a great job of adding color and flavor to the individual NPCs as they interact. There's enough to keep track of already, so make your life easier by only tracking the allies, villains and patrons of your world. —JF not mutually exclusive—you can have a villainous patron, or an ally who turns on the party if their goals don't align—but it's not likely an NPC will be functioning in more than one of these roles for very long, and it's easier to discuss them as separate ideas in theory, even if the lines get a little blurry in practice.

ALLIES

Allies fill an important niche in tabletop games. They are essentially companions: willing, friendly (or at least helpful) NPCs that provide the characters a measure of assistance. But allies vary widely in function. They serve a vast array of purposes, none of which fit neatly into a single box. Ensuring you get the most out of each ally you present starts with defining what an ally is and why they're important to your game.

Allies are characters who choose to work with your heroes because their goals align with the party's in the short or long term. Allies will generally step into the arena as willing companions, but most importantly, they work with the characters as beneficial partners. They are equals—not necessarily in power, but from the perspective of a job. They don't work for the players, at least not in the way an underling does. If a player's goals change, an ally might leave the party to go do their own thing, whereas an underling is obliged to stay with the party regardless of the story's course.

To better understand the distinction between an ally and other types of NPCs, let's take a look at an example of an ally in fiction: Beorn from *The Hobbit*. Beorn is a shapeshifter who takes on the visage of a bear. His existence is relatively peaceful with one small exception: the goblins nearby are a thorn in his side. He despises goblins and hopes to be rid of them. He has the mid-term goal of "eliminate the approaching goblin menace." When Bilbo, Thorin and the other protagonists arrive, they have just completed their short-term goal of "defeat and escape the goblins chasing us" by slaying the Goblin King and a few of his followers. This has furthered Beorn's goal, and he realizes his goals align with the party's. This prompts him to provide benefits to the party, including lodging, food and steeds for their journey.

Allies can serve a broad variety of purposes based on their skills and, more importantly, their goals. If an ally has the goal of "Slay the local tyrant," they may be more inclined to assist the players in battle itself to see this goal completed. Gaining allies, and making them useful without robbing the players' sense of accomplishment, is the biggest challenge of running allied NPCs effectively.

GAINING ALLIES

Characters need to gain allies before they can enjoy the benefits of an alliance. Just as leveling up comes from XP and gear comes from gold, rewards can also come in the form of allies, a storytelling device that is often underutilized. Allies provide tangible in-game benefits

---

HEROES

I use the term "hero" a lot when describing the PCs. Please don't misunderstand me—I don't mean the characters are necessarily good, only that they are the primary characters. I use the word to emphasize that they are the driving force of our story, not that they're heroic knights saving the innocents before them. Conan the Barbarian was a hero, but he was not what RPG enthusiasts might call "Lawful Good." He doesn't adhere to any recognizable set of morals. He was the central character, he was a driver of plot and he was the one we were rooting for, but that didn't make him Sir Galahad the Pure, nor did it need to. —*TF*

and letting players earn them as a result of challenging circumstances can be a reward that also advances your table's story.

The most common form of ally is the impromptu recruit. The players want to recruit some little goblin they find eating a chicken in the dungeon. Great. How does that work, exactly? Remember that allies want to follow the characters, but they need aligned goals in order to do so. The goals of a potential ally don't need to be precisely the same as the player goals (although this is fine) but they do need to align with one another.

If, for example, the players want to raid the nearby fort of their sworn enemy and the goblin is looking to overthrow his old master, their goals align. This goal-driven partnership keeps the players from trying to befriend every enemy they face. A goblin raiding a village will likely not forsake its family, lords and gods to slave away under a ragtag band of adventurers, since their goals don't align at all, but a hopeless mercenary lost in the wilderness might be willing to team up in order to fulfill their "return to civilization" short-term goal, simply to take advantage of the safety to be found in numbers.

You can also create an NPC for the express purpose of being an ally—a kindly shopkeep who could use a few friends or a warrior seeking strong companions. These types of allies are fine; they can be refreshing and fun to roleplay. But these aren't capital A Allies in the categorical sense used here. They lack the dedication to a cause that true allies have, and therefore have less utility in a game. An NPC who is the party's ally simply because they've been nice won't fight for the party like one who shares the party's goals or has defined goals of their own (which complement the party's). When you plan to create an ally, make sure the players have goals that properly align with those of the NPC instead of passing reasons to be friendly to one another. Buying a lonely old codger a horn of ale might mean he'll help you find an object that fulfills your short-term goal, but we can't expect him to follow the heroes into battle against an army of the damned. If an NPC needs some new, influential adventurers in town to talk to the local lord on their behalf (to work at fulfilling a goal of "secure a sizable grant from my local ruler") and the players have a related goal ("Find a good reason to infiltrate the lord's castle") then the two can form a partnership. Give and take can lead to a beautiful friendship, on occasion.

From a proactive perspective, allies can arise from nearly anywhere. When the players seek out a specific character in hopes of becoming their ally, not only are they firmly taking the reins of the story, but they can expect what to get out of the situation and pursue their goals accordingly. Characters who need an army to reclaim their home may venture to the Forbidden Keep of the Unkillable Warlord while players that hope to learn a secret piece of lore may go to the Grand Librarian. The possibilities are endless, but the table on pg. 82 can

LOSING ALLIES

Unlike other rewards, allies generally require some upkeep to hang on to. I will often remind players that allies are characters in their own right and are pursuing their own goals. Even if they've helped the party in the past, that's no guarantee they will in the future. An ally with whom the party has a good relationship might help them just because they are friends, but not forever. If the party's goals conflict with the ally's, that could mean tension or outright hostility, even if they've worked together in the past. I also tell my players an alliance is a two-way street: If the ally is in need and the party doesn't help them, they risk losing that relationship. This is a great narrative hook to get players involved in something they wouldn't otherwise dabble in, which is a convenient way for me to introduce new characters and locations. —JF help spur your ally creation along.

So, the party has gained a brand new, super cool, exciting ally! Boblin the Goblin is ready to roll! Except now, the players want Boblin to help them in every way possible. The players keep Boblin around. Boblin takes up a turn in combat. Boblin is the meat shield for traps. Boblin uses all the magical gear the party outgrows. And poor, poor Boblin is now a full-time adventurer. This can take a toll on a GM and bog down the game, especially with a group that loves to make friends. The solution? Boblin leaves. "Thanks for the memories! And the gear! I'm off to find my family!" And that's it. When the ally gets what they want (and not, it should be stated, what the party wants), the ally can simply walk away. The transaction is complete.

An ally is only an ally when the specific, concrete goals that fuel proactive play overlap between NPC and player. While the relationship between your adventurers and their new ally can blossom into a real friendship, this doesn't equate to an ally assisting in the completion of their goals. Allies can naturally diverge from the characters when goals disappear, although "fulfill my debt to my new friends" can certainly be a new short- or mid-term goal for an ally.

ALLY GOALS

Like the PCs (and, as discussed soon, villains and patrons) allies have goals of their own. One of each type of goal—long, medium and short—often suffices, which you can flesh out or improvise as you please. These goals should naturally overlap with the party's, making for a natural and proactive partnership. If you're having trouble thinking of aligned ally goals, use the table below for inspiration.

Player Goal	Aligned Goal
Avenge the death of a loved one.	Slay the local tyrant.
Recover a secret spell lost to time.	Locate a mystical lost library.
Discover the true identity of an important person.	Uncover a political scandal.
Slay a powerful monster.	Use the heart of the same powerful monster to make a disease-curing potion for themselves.
Discover the location of a fabled natural feature.	Extract a magical metal from fabled natural feature.
Claim an ancestral birthright or fortune.	Cast out the current monarchy.
Conduct a grand ritual or spell that would cause a huge positive effect.	Benefit from the positive effect (such as the curing of a disease, resurrection of a loved one, etc.).
Kill a god.	Reclaim a lost soul taken by this god.

DESIGNING ALLIES

Once you have your goals, you can begin designing the ally as a proper NPC. While doing so, consider the following questions to shape their personality, methods of pursuing their goal and overall usefulness to the players (in short, what can they offer the party that the party wouldn't otherwise have?).

1. Goal Alignment: How closely do the ally's goals align with those of the players? If they diverge, could it cause conflict? If they align perfectly, does it make the ally favor the players? If the goals change or collide, how does the ally react?

2. Method of Pursuit: How does the ally fulfill their goals? Do they attempt to use violence? Are they charming? How do they behave in combat, if they engage at all? How about in a tense negotiation?

3. Allied Factions: Do your players know groups or individuals related to this ally? Are they on good terms? What issues are they involved in relevant to other goals? Does this affect how far an ally will go to help them?

LETTING PLAYERS SHINE

Placing NPCs in combat situations, at least in 5e and similar games, will slow the fight down. It's unavoidable. Game Masters have plenty to worry about already, and there's no need to add even more moving parts. Additionally, giving players allies without the fictional, and thus more malleable, character outshining them is easier said than done—it's easy for an NPC to steal the spotlight. Ideally, the ally is less powerful than the players but provides help via resources to which the players lack access.

Is the party composed of melee fighters? Maybe their old friend Boblin is a healer or magic user. Lots of squishy players? Perhaps Boblin is a tank. But most of all, an ally's turn should be the shortest by far. Under no circumstances should you be using hefty stat blocks from a book. Allies should do one thing, and one thing only. Maybe they know two or three spells, perhaps a few swings of the sword, and then they're done. These are not PCs or monsters—give them just enough bells and whistles to play a particular note over and over and call it a day.

You'll know when the group has an ally and can adjust encounter difficulty accordingly. Allies should feel useful—otherwise, what's the point?—but their utility should not pull the spotlight from the heroes. From a combat perspective, they assist, but should not inflict as much damage as the party. Allies must not be more important than the characters. Taking into account the concepts introduced in Chapter 1, these are bit players, not A-listers. An important ally can evolve and even grow in power as the PCs do (otherwise they'll lose their utility), but they shouldn't eclipse the party as far as their power level is concerned (barring exceptions that might benefit the overall arc of your story).

Allies also need to act in accordance with their goals in combat. An

CASE STUDY

Balurium

An example of a successful ally in a campaign is Balurium Violeteyes, a minstrel my party picked up at a carnival in a 5e campaign. The group hired the musician to sing of their glories across the lands and follow them at times to gather materials for his songs. Eventually, the bard grew fond of his new companions and decided to assist them when he could.

Balurium worked as an ally for three reasons: he was a scarce presence, simple and cowardly (but loyal nonetheless). His scarcity was key: Balurium was not a pest. He was there when the party wanted him to be and sometimes wasn't even if they did. He would show up for travels now and again, then go back to his own devices. His mechanics were simple and therefore perfect. He had a fixed Initiative score and could only do two things: make an attack and give Bardic Inspiration a few times a day. I would roll all his dice at once and his turn would conclude in 10 seconds, quick and easy. Finally, he was cowardly. This doesn't mean he ran away—that would make him traitorous, worse than a coward. He would bemoan circumstances, advise the players away from threats, was clearly not as powerful as his companions and never wildly attempted to charge a dragon and sacrifice himself. He wasn't the hero—the players were. They felt powerful with Balurium, and panicked whenever he came close to death. He reinforced their role as heroes. —*TF* ally whose goal is to slay a certain enemy will likely not knock them unconscious. Consider the goal itself—is it violent in nature? Is death on the line? Is it deeply related to the current situation? Use these goals as cues to reinforce the proactive nature of the encounters allies take part in. If Boblin has the long-term goal "save my wife," he may prioritize releasing her from her bonds over fighting her captor in the final climactic battle.

VILLAINS

Possibly the most vital of any of the NPCs you create, a good villain is unique because of the specific way their goals interact with PC goals. Just like the players, villains have goals, agency and plans (not to mention minions). But unlike player goals, villains should have goals (and plans to achieve them) that overlap in some way with those of the players. Of course, these plans could potentially spread far and wide—the mighty dragon's plans range across the continent!—but their machinations should be felt by the heroes, even in their lowliest days of adventuring.

Examples in fantasy include Sauron from *The Lord of the Rings*, The Dark One from *The Wheel of Time* and Odium from *The Stormlight Archive*. Each of these villains had massive, world-spanning plans that were felt by the heroes of these stories in their earliest days. Sauron's servants ravaged Middle-earth, and Frodo and his compatriots feel the rumblings of Mordor all the way in the Shire. As they travel, they find kingdoms beaten down by orcs, kings possessed by evil and most of all, they struggle against one tiny golden ring. Nearly every challenge they face stems in some way from Sauron, sowing the seeds of conquest across the continent. He wants to conquer the free peoples of Middle-earth, and the Fellowship of the Ring wants to stay free: conflicting goals in broad forms.

Villains will change in their presentation, setting, power level and personality, but their relationship with the party should be one of conflict, which arises from opposing goals. Like the rank-and-file minions that heroes face in their adventures, they present the heroes with obstacles, but unlike such enemies, they have agency and greater goals. But unlike in classic fantasy, that agency is a facade. In proactive fantasy, the villains form and pursue goals in response to the goals that players have designed.

Creating a Villain

Villains are not created equal, nor should they be. When designing a villain, a GM must ask themselves what their setting is, what the players are hoping for and what you as a GM believe the players are most likely to engage with on a story level. No villain is the same, but most possess the following traits:

1. Villainous. This one seems obvious, but you might be surprised. We use the term villainous instead of evil because many GMs create torn, morally ambiguous villains who almost seem like anti-heroes. There is absolutely nothing wrong with this. I have seen some incredible games with morally complex villains. But each one was run by a highly experienced GM, and we can count the times it's worked well on one hand. We prefer fairly antagonists who are knowingly evil, villains that are very clearly villainous. Moral ambiguity is not what makes a villain interesting; introducing a figure of unquestionable evil does not make the story boring. Being clearly evil doesn't mean the villain has no understandable motives or relatable traits, but what they do should be almost objectively evil. They need to be doing something that conflicts with PC goals and offers some opposing

Cyvernith

Sometimes the best way to explain the right way to do something is to start by explaining how to do it wrong. In my earliest days of running games, I created Cyvernith, a mighty dragon. His long-term goal was...well, he didn't exactly have one aside from "defeat the heroes" and "rule all the land." Vague and imprecise. Additionally, I was still stuck in the mindset of reactionary play—the dragon would act, and the players would be forced to respond. But when even the villain lacks clear plans, the game loses its tension and excitement, and players quickly become bored and frustrated. Cyvernith and a couple of goblins attacked some farmers until the heroes showed up and slew him in a cornfield. There were no connections, no stakes and no reason for the characters to do it other than "we are heroes." But in a later campaign, I brought back Cyvernith, this time with clear goals and connections related to the heroes. His goal was to conquer a certain city and plunder it for his hoard. To this end, he had connections to the heroes (including a dragon sorcerer, always a godsend for a connection to a dragon) and specific minions, plans and goals that linked him to the heroes. Instead of "defeat the heroes" his goal was "control the ruler of the city in secret," a goal that conflicted with another player's plan to rule the city himself. A little definition goes a long way in creating a more enjoyable game for you and your players. —*TF*

view of the world, or the story lacks conflict. And conflict is what drives most stories.

2. Powerful. This one is subjective to the power of the players, but a villain should be a threat. Whether physically, mentally, politically or otherwise, the villain should be able to harm the heroes. The cunning mage not only has incredible magical power but a keen intellect, a penchant for brutal traps and a massive network of criminals throughout the city. A mighty dragon is more than just its scorching breath of fire. Leverage its cleverness and tenacity, its horde of minions and its great magical knowledge and/or wealth. All villains should have great power of some sort; otherwise, why should the heroes even bother charging into battle themselves? This doesn't mean every villain is a massive, world-ending threat but that relative to the strength of the heroes they should hold great power. For new adventurers, the nearby hobgoblin warlord is a terrifying foe. To close out a three-year campaign, a mighty necromancer ascending to godhood may be more appropriate.

3. Goal-Driven. This is the most important aspect of the villain from the proactive player perspective. You must design villain goals with players in mind. These specific, concrete goals must overlap with those of the heroes in some way, shape or form or you'll find your villain will never interest them. The specific goals of your villains are tangible ways your heroes will do battle with them. While "villainous" defines what these goals will be, "goal-driven" ensures villains work proactively.

VILLAINOUS GOALS

GMs will occasionally feel an urge to design villains objectively, choosing their goals exclusively for whatever they believe is the most likely plan in the context of their world. Resist this urge. Villain goals cannot be designed the same way as player goals. There are similarities, yes, but villains serve a different function than heroes, and their goals must reflect that.

Villains need to be designed through the lens of the characters. Remember, in our ideal proactive game, the villains are made in response to the characters' actions to tie them together, and only then do they begin acting proactively. Looking at the scope of each goal, we can begin to see the workings of a villain.

1. Long-Term: the true scope of the villain. Your villain should always have a concrete goal, just like the players. While most goals should be specific and tangible, villains can afford to be a touch more vague with their long-term goal, at least until later into the game. Their goals can always be achievable since you design their power, resources and avenues to pursue this goal. Think in specifics. While a long-term villain goal could be "Conquer the land," all this really achieves is more concrete mid-term goals than usual. "Crush the capital of the nation into rubble" and "Publicly execute the king" work far better. "Become very powerful" is different from "Break the seals on the ancient tome, using it to ascend to godhood," and we'll leave you to guess which one you think we prefer. The guidelines we introduced in Chapter 1 continue to work here, but keep in mind that your villain's goals have additional restrictions based on their overall alignment, as well as the fact that they must be so dastardly that they garner the attention of up-and-coming heroes who are seeking out goals of their own. The greater goal should be a threat that affects many people, especially the main heroes, or else there is no reason to stop them.

2. Mid-Term: goals that affect smaller areas. Same as with PC goals, a villain's mid-term goals are stepping stones to their larger aim, but will

MAKING YOUR VILLAIN HATEABLE

Now of course, some players will pursue a villain because it's the right thing to do. Some will do so because of deep-seated aspects of the story ("The villain is terrorizing my hometown!" "Yes, and he's holding my father captive!" "Yes, and he's also my father!"). Beyond a story and mechanics, however, there should be a reason why your players want to defeat your villain (and therefore why killing or otherwise defeating them feels so good): they just hate the guy (or gal! Or risen deity!). When a villain is despicable, it feels good to beat them, and it provides a better reason to pursue their defeat. How do we achieve this? By utilizing a villain's goal to tamper with a character's goal. Sacred god? Bespoiled and desecrated. Beloved ally? Kidnapped and killed. Bought a home? Sundered and turned into a White Castle. Giving the characters specific reasons to hate your villain makes it feel that much better when they finally bite the dust. —*TF* still comprise numerous short term goals which, once completed, will lead them closer to where they want to be (on the throne; ascending to godhood; immortal but also rich). A villain's mid-term goals are the battlefields upon which most of the party's conflict with the villain will unfold. Having minions pursue these goals, perhaps led by a particularly powerful follower of some kind, is a common strategy. "Seize control of the village" is a decent goal, and sending Grolar the Mighty with his horde of goblins to do so is an excellent threat to the heroes. Mid-term goals, however, should generate several shorter-term goals that provide specific encounters, depending on our player's actions. If a villain's mid-term goal is "Seize control of all the area's diamond mines," to support a long term goal of "Create a monopoly on revivifying magic," then the short term goals of "take over diamond mines 1-5 by any means necessary" immediately present themselves.

BORROWING CLICHÉS

Tristan and I agree cliches can be useful, but I take it to another level. In one of my GMing binders, I have a page that's covered with all the movie plots I think would make interesting encounters or goals. I write them in a way that's vague (see if you can spot the movie!): "a group of soldiers is stalked by a powerful monster in the wilderness," "a hero is accidentally trapped in a hostage situation," "an isolated group of people is infiltrated by a shapeshifter," etc. I can adapt these plots to many situations, and when I'm out of ideas, I consult the list for inspiration. Since I'm changing the setting and often tweaking one or two small things about them, they don't feel like total rip-offs. My players, being players, have never once noticed that they are playing through the plot of a popular movie. Fantastic conflicts and interesting encounters are all around you. Use them! —JF

3. Short-Term: goals that provide encounters. These are the meat and potatoes of your big bads, where the heroes can actually interact with your villain's machinations in real-time through discourse, negotiations, puzzles or punches to the face. Generating encounters is too subjective a process to write in massive detail about, but getting to the point where the concepts blossom naturally is a key aspect of short-term goals. Each short-term goal should be small enough in scale that it can have a few encounters built around it. If our villain has the mid-term goal of "Level the town," short-term goals can emerge that both achieve this and create interesting encounters. "Destroy the prison walls," "Burn city hall," "Crush the militia" and "Execute the mayor" are all quick, short-term goals that both facilitate the mid-term goal and provide inspiration for potential encounters. These goals form the bulk of plans, and creating these are essential to interaction with the heroes.

Bear in mind, as long as you are not publicly announcing your villain's every intent, you are not bound to the goals you create. You can (and probably should) change goals, editing them to better suit your group, promote interesting play and generate better encounters as your games progress and your party explores more of the story together. This also helps when players go in an unexpected direction (common in a proactive game) and keeps your villain relevant. Additionally, creating new short- or mid-term goals (and, if necessary, long-term ones) is an essential part of running a villain—they'll adapt to situations, establish new goals and craft new plans. If you're struggling to find goals for your villains, try using the table that follows for inspiration. Each villain goal is tied in some way to character goals.

Character Goal	Villain Goal
Be crowned king in a coronation ceremony.	Destroy the kingdom's capital.
Destroy the One Ring.	Wield the One Ring to conquer the world.
Discover the location of a fabled geographical feature.	Seize the feature for magical benefits.
Defend an important young person.	Raise the young person to mold them into a weapon.
Discover their own identity as an important person.	Brainwash the person to steal a station that should rightfully be the hero's.
Learn an important secret that was locked away.	Maintain exclusive access to the secret, using it for personal gain.
Return to their homeland.	Conquer the homeland, becoming emperor.
Conduct a grand ritual or spell that would cause a huge positive effect.	Tamper with the use of magic in the kingdom, leaving it helpless against invading forces.

CONNECTIONS TO CHARACTERS

A key aspect of villain goals is how they overlap with character goals. This doesn't mean goals are built around the characters, merely that they conflict over areas of common interest. For major conflict, actual character goals should overlap directly with villain goals, while for more coincidental conflict, geographical, political, familial and other connections can overlap.

Connections to players through essential aspects of character motivation are simpler to set up. Why does my character care about this villain? Well, they're attacking the town you're in right now. Geography and location work perfectly fine as inciting incidents and occasionally set up further conflict, representing baby steps toward deeper connections. There's a reason a character being related to the villain

Dralthakar the Rotting

Having shared an ineffective villain in Cyrnevith (pg. 87), I wanted to detail an antagonist that exemplifies our approach (and also has a cool name). Dralthakar was a mighty lich, attempting to ascend to godhood and crush the world beneath his boots. He was the BBEG in a massive campaign run in 5e, spanning from level 1 to 20, so the group saw a ton of this guy over the course of play. I created Dralkthakar before Jonah shared his concept of goal-driven characters and villains with me, but we were both already subconsciously using these concepts. Dralthakar was no exception. Labeling his goals looking back (and noticing how they conflicted with player goals), I would define his long-term goal as "Obtain this magical artifact and ascend to godhood" (conflicting with "Earn a great boon from my god") and some of his mid-term goals as "Seize the capital of this fief" (conflicting with "Become a fief lord"), "Open mass tunnels from the surface to monstrous caves" (against "Defeat the encroaching army of monsters") and "Manipulate the king into destroying the land for me" (against "Protect my father, the king"). These are all still fairly vague, but as a key villain with plans on plans, most of the specifics were handled by lower-level, close-to-the-ground goals. For example, "Siphon corpses from the graveyard to build an army of undead" led to multiple encounters with the party.

Evil goals aside, the characters hated Dralthakar—not in a frustrated or irritating way but because he was a perfect figure to despise. He slew their friends, resurrected their corpses as undead and sent them after the characters as assassins. He led the party into traps, destroyed their homes and forced them into conflicts that spelled certain doom. Dralthakar was a terrifying figure, and with fingers in every pie in the land, the players encountered his machinations frequently, setting them up to create a new goal: Put an end to Dralthakar for good. —*TF*

is such a common trope. It's perfect! It adds conflict, drama, tension and a clear link between protagonist and antagonist. Is it cliché? A bit. I certainly wouldn't encourage you to seek out clichés, but there's often a reason they've become so popular, and a good GM can find a way to twist them just enough to feel fresh while still retaining the core aspect of what makes them so useful in the first place.

Creating goals that overlap seems easy, but there's a bit more under the hood than one would expect. If the players are constantly pursuing the exact same objectives as the villain, it can quickly become a frustrating slog. Because of this, it's important to add twists, subversions and complications that change the dynamic between goals a bit. Instead of "I want to take this god's magical symbol" as a goal for both a character and a villain, perhaps that is only the player's goal, while the villain has "I want to kill the priests so that the village has no healers" as a midterm goal with a few specific methods of attack under it as shorter ones. This way, it isn't a game of tug-of-war, but instead a more interesting and dynamic form of conflict. Ideally, when the players interact with a villain this way, encounters result naturally as conflict emerges.

PATRONS

Patrons are the archetypal quest-givers, the wealthy and powerful NPCs whose work behind the scenes and support for the PCs make many of their adventures possible. In proactive fantasy games, patrons serve more as resources and enablers than as proper NPCs. Think of a patron as an NPC that players can utilize to pursue their goals, as opposed to an ally, who actually shares the players' goals. Patrons almost never appear in the field, and in some cases, the adventurers they patronize may rarely even meet them. Patrons can represent nearly any faction, from monarchs who lead governments to crime bosses of the city underworld to high priests of a fallen god, but they are usually highly placed in their respective factions. Examples of patrons in classical fantasy include Elrond of Rivendell in *The Lord of the Rings* and Queen Morgase of Andor in *The Wheel of Time*.

Patrons Aren't Allies

While both patrons and allies are NPCs the players might think of as friendly, they are not the same thing. A patron is a character that might not share the party's goals but may decide to help them pursue their goals anyway, enabling the PCs to work harder, better or faster. This aid isn't free: in exchange, the patron expects the party to advance the patron's own plans, knowingly or not.

A patron provides the resources the player characters need in order to tackle challenges beyond themselves. Securing the support of a patron can be a big power boost for player characters, and obtaining a suitable patron (or more suitable—AKA wealthier—if they already have one) could be an appropriate player goal in and of itself.

Contrast this function with the function of an ally, who serves as a supporting character in the story. Allies often provide guidance to certain areas, very particular powers or access to certain people in a way that rounds out the player characters' powers. Allies do not represent a resource pool that the player characters may tap into as a way to further their agendas—but patrons do.

Additionally, the power dynamic between a patron and the PCs is not balanced. Due to their power and prestige, a patron has a social status higher than the PCs, treating them accordingly. The patron likely has other adventurers to patronize and is probably unwilling to put up with much disrespect or incompetence from the player characters. Contrast this again with an ally, whose goals align with one or more party members and is therefore working with the player characters out of necessity, common purpose, shared ideology or some other reason that puts them on common ground.

When introducing a patron, keep these two factors (patrons grant power; patrons have more authority than the party) in mind. Patrons,

and the conditions of their patronage, are one of the guardrails your
players will bump up against in their proactive goal-chasing and can be
a good tool for you to encourage certain behaviors in play if you need
to correct the party's course without outright railroading your players.
A patron might help your characters chase goals that are currently
beyond their means, but only if they follow the conditions the patron
saddles them with. This creates interesting dynamics that allow the PCs
to play with powers and capabilities that come at a cost.

Designing Patrons

The patrons you introduce should represent one of the factions you
have already designed. They may be the leader, or they may simply be
in a position of power relative to the players. The patron will be able
to offer the players some of the resources of the faction, provided the
players can help the patron advance their own goals. When designing
a patron, think about the following factors to place your patron in the
setting and make them a good resource for future encounter-building.

1. What resources does your patron's faction have? This may
come in the form of wealth, but could also be other resources: information, technology, manpower, etc. You'll need to know this in order

to figure out what your player characters will gain by working with (read: for) the patron, but you'll also need it later to help develop a preferred goal-seeking style of the patron. The head of a clan of assassins will tackle problems very differently than the leader of a wealthy merchant's guild. Knowing the resources your patron wields helps determine how they'll act in a given situation.

2. How powerful is your patron's faction relative to the other factions in your setting? Decide which challenges your patron is equipped to handle, which goals are beneath them and exactly how much power your player characters are getting their hands on—as well as just how difficult or dangerous the tasks the patron might require of them will be. After all, if the faction is particularly powerful, why

WHY WE DESIGN PATRON PERSONALITY FIRST

Unlike allies and villains, who we usually design by keeping players' goals in mind first and filling in personality details for later, we design patrons with their personalities first, and fill in details about their goals based on the players' goals later. This is the same approach we use for factions, and its purpose is to balance the feeling of a sandbox world versus a world on rails. If every character the players meet just so happens to be interested in the same things they are, the world feels like it revolves around the party and will only change in response to their actions. If we want to create a world that feels alive and dynamic, we need to have some actors that are pursuing their own goals and changing the world regardless of—possibly even indifferent to—the players' actions. This is the role patrons and their factions fill in our games. As powerful individuals and organizations, patrons and factions can pursue their own goals regardless of whether the players help them or not, which means the world will change and advance with or without the players' help. —*JF* wouldn't they just do the job themselves?

3. What are the general personality traits of your patron? We'll use this to help develop specific goals later. A patron will pursue goals in accordance with their personality. You don't need to get specific or deep here—a simple list of two or three adjectives like greedy, ambitious or generous will do.

For each of the above considerations, think about the ways in which your patron is an expression of the faction they belong to—a certain aspect of your faction personified. They'll inherit their resources and power level from their faction (with a few modifications, if they don't lead the faction outright), and you can design their personality traits to reflect the ideology of their faction. If the faction's ideology is merciless, for example, the patron might be cruel, just or apathetic; if the faction's ideology is generous, the patron might be kind, selfless or even gluttonous.

LONG-TERM PATRON GOALS

Once you have outlined your patron NPC based on the criteria established previously, you can start generating specific long-term goals for your patron. It's easiest to create only long-term goals for patrons at first, working in the background toward those goals and only occasionally measuring direct progress. Generate short-term goals for the patron when the player characters are involved and want help from the patron—this ensures you can create a short-term goal for the patron that will involve the party in the way you want it to. If you decide on the short-term goals ahead of time, it's too difficult to predict how you can work them into the ever-changing story you're telling with your players.

Generate your long-term goals for your patron by looking at their resources, power level and ideology. What would someone with that set of things want? Do they want to expand their control, wealth or access? Do they want to diminish that of a rival? Do they want to leverage the resources they have in service of their ideology? If you're having trouble with this part of patron creation, consider using the table at right for ideas. To use the table, roll 1d10 to find a long-term goal. Next, choose from the options in the parentheses to customize the goal to fit your patron's personality. Alternatively, you can roll on the PC goal table in Chapter 1 for more fleshed-out player goals.

1d10	Patron Goal
1	Expand their network of (wealth/information/prestige/military power).
2	Enforce a claim on property or land that is (legitimate/illegitimate/questionable).
3	Uncover a secret about a rival through (subterfuge/diplomacy/bribery).
4	Get revenge against someone who wronged them for a (petty/serious/fake) reason.
5	Provide (no-strings-attached/many-strings-attached) aid to an ally in need.
6	Gain an ally through (military alliance/diplomacy/blackmail/trade).
7	Obtain an item that (is lost/belongs to someone/hasn't been created yet).
8	Complete a magical (ritual/spell/sacrifice) to (empower themselves/aid someone).
9	Claim a position of power through (legal/illegal) means.
10	Personally profit from a (disaster/trade deal/secret being exposed/war).

Once you have a long-term patron goal, you can generate mid-and short-term goals on an as-needed basis. These short-term goals will still be based on the patron's ideology and power level, but you can custom-design them for the situation the party is in to create the greatest impact. It's unlikely a patron's long-term goals will intersect with the players in an exciting way since the long-term goals are generated without the players in mind. But when the players seek out a patron, or when you feel the patron should get involved, you can plan the perfect short-term goal for your patron to make their interests collide with the party's.

SHORT-TERM PATRON GOALS

A patron's short-term goal should be generated when the party wants to pursue a goal that is out of reach for them, or when they could use some additional help or firepower. The party is supported by the patron's resources and the patron makes progress toward a long-term goal in exchange. It's important to not generate these short-term goals ahead of time, since it's hard to predict what direction the party will take with a particular goal, so stay flexible. When the party needs help, it's time to generate a short-term goal for the interested patron.

When using a patron in this way, remember that a patron who wants exactly what the party wants is really just a power boost disguised as narrative (and is sort of boring to boot). Drama comes from characters with opposing or not-quite-aligning goals that clash as they both seek to achieve their aims, so choose a short-term goal for your patron that aligns imperfectly with the short-term goals of the party.

The easiest way to do this is to make your patron's short-term goal a simple variation on the party's short-term goal: a reframing of that short-term goal such that it serves the patron's plans better. This can be a simple exchange, like claiming a share of loot in exchange for help, or it can be the beginning of a longer relationship. To use the table that follows, find a PC short-term goal listed on the table (or roll randomly for one if you can't decide which goal you'd like the party to have a patron getting involved in). Next, read the related patron goals. Pick a patron you have created with this long-term goal or a similar one.

Finally, read the patron's negotiation: This is what the patron should ask for in exchange for their help. It will allow the players to complete their short-term goal but serve the patron's plans at the same time.

PC Short-Term Goals	Patron Related Goals	Patron Negotiations
Obtain a certain magic item, hidden knowledge or access to a certain important person.	Expand their network of (wealth/information/ prestige/military power).	Ownership of magic item with rental rights to the party, shared hidden knowledge or introduction to an important person.
Delve into a dangerous location, establish a base of operations.	Enforce a claim on property or land that is (legitimate/illegitimate/ questionable).	A certain item from the dangerous location, ownership of or economic stake in the base of operations.
Gain an invitation to an elite social gathering, gain access to a restricted area.	Uncover a secret about a rival through (subterfuge/ diplomacy/bribery).	Spy on a rival, plant a bug or secret agent in the restricted area.
Eliminate a powerful enemy, collect a bounty.	Get revenge against someone who wronged them for a (petty/serious/ fake) reason.	Conceal patron's involvement, split the bounty.
Prove devotion to a god, protect an important person, keep an important promise.	Provide (no-strings-attached/many-strings-attached) aid to an ally in need.	Claim responsibility for the party's action to impress someone important, collect payment for aid.
Escort someone through dangerous territory, gather harmful information on someone important, transport a valuable item.	Gain an ally through (military alliance/ diplomacy/blackmail/ trade).	Claim a favor from receivers of person, have blackmail information shared with them, gain trading rights or favorable terms with receivers of item.

Locate or obtain a certain magic item, locate a craftsman.	Obtain an item that (is lost/belongs to someone/ hasn't been created yet).	Ownership of the item with rental rights to party, favorable production deal with the craftsman.
Learn a magic spell or ritual, locate or aid a certain spellcaster, access certain arcane or occult knowledge.	Complete a magical (ritual/spell/sacrifice) to (empower themselves/ aid someone).	Share details of spell or ritual, gain access or introduction to spellcaster, ownership of arcane or occult knowledge.
Gain favor with local faction, harm or topple local faction.	Claim a position of power through (legal/ illegal) means.	Party's good word or referral to faction, party's support in taking over harmed or toppled faction.
Aid disaster victims, make a trade deal, blackmail someone important, start or stop a war.	Personally profit from a (disaster/trade deal/secret being exposed/war).	Disaster relief contract guarantees, favorable trade deal terms, access to blackmail information, choice of first conflict site.

Unlike an ally, a patron's aid usually isn't free. When the player characters come to the patron seeking help, the patron can bargain with them, giving them what they seek in exchange for something else. You have two dials to tune when you set up the negotiation this way: the aid the patron is willing to give, from none up to the full measure of their resources and the restrictions they will impose on their aid, from none up to full compliance with their ideology and alignment with their long-term goals. Adjust these dials in tandem, with greater resources available to parties who are willing to adhere more completely to the patron's ideology and/or who go out of their way to help the patron accomplish their goals. Use your patrons to help players tackle those player goals that are a bit out of their current reach—just make sure the patron is getting what they want in return.

CASE STUDY

Constable Harburk

The third official campaign published for the 5e is famously obtuse. I've tried to run it three times now and only the third attempt went well. I believe it's because I used the principles of proactive fantasy outlined in this book. My interpretation of the dull but good-hearted Constable Harburk is a prime example of why. In my interpretation of *Princes of the Apocalypse*, Harburk runs a militia group (the Town Watch faction) in Red Larch and works out of the back of the butcher shop. This tells me three things: he has access to manpower and maybe food, he is weaker than the town council faction but stronger than anyone else in town and he generally wants to protect the town and keep the peace (resources, power level and personality, respectively, from the guidelines above). Notice how I could easily determine Harburk's access to resources and power level from his faction affiliation: since I'd planned the factions out beforehand, I could have improvised any one of the NPCs affiliated with it, rather than creating all of them one-by-one.

I decided my Constable Harburk was shrewd, kind-hearted and blunt. This personality decision allowed me to take the Town Watch faction's goal of keeping the peace and transform it into Harburk's long-term goal of "restore the safety of Red Larch to the way it was when I was a boy," which is a personal take on a classic town guard goal. I introduced Harburk as a patron after the players told a story in the tavern about being attacked by bandits—I had him approach them the next day and ask a few questions about the attack. He offered them some provisions and the aid of his small militia to go back after the bandits, provided they bring him the bandit leader, known as Long Jim, alive. Later, he offered to aid the party in investigating the attacks in the quarry, but any perpetrators were to be brought to him, unharmed, so the town could put them on trial.

Notice an important distinction here: Harburk approached the characters in reaction to an adventure of theirs and offered them aid in something they wanted to do anyway, but weren't able to accomplish at their current level. He facilitated their goal of getting revenge on the bandits, then was available as a resource after that. Whenever the characters wanted to do something they thought would benefit the safety of the town, they could usually count on Harburk to lend his support. I could use Harburk's presence in town and knowledge of the area to point them toward interesting dungeons in the vicinity, but I rarely used him as an explicit quest-giver after the first introduction. —*JF*

Mr. Krahal

As one of the favorite villains I've ever run, Mr. Krahal deserves
a special mention on my patrons examples list. In a Blades in the
Dark game (and most TTRPGs, really), one of the worst things
you can do is to make a deal with a demon: Mr. Krahal was my
attempt at exploring this side of the game. I introduced Mr. Krahal
(real name unknown, "Krahal" reminded me of "Crawling Chaos")
in the middle of an unrelated adventure, when the characters
were breaking into the warehouses of a reclusive, utterly insane
warlock. Bombs were used, a basement collapsed and a magic circle
confining Mr. Krahal was broken.

In return for the freedom the characters granted him, Mr. Krahal
helped the characters escape and get to safety. As a demon, his
goals were unknowable to them, and they wisely kept their distance.
But as he began to establish himself in the city and repurpose an
existing cult to his own ends (in this case, he changed the faction's
goals to match his own), the characters began to see more of him.
He often heard of their exploits and sent his encouragements,
along with an offer of aid if they should need it. His long-term goal,
unknown to the players, was to resurrect the corpse of a long-
dead sea demon trapped beneath the city, and he needed some
powerful artifacts and hidden information to do it. The cult he
had commandeered, now a major faction in the city, had access to
impressive resources and knowledge and were more powerful than
many of the other fringe religious groups in the city. This allowed
Mr. Krahal to pursue his goals mostly unimpeded.

But since the players were targeting his enemies anyway, he sent
weapons, money and other gifts to help them accomplish their
goals, asking only for a few small bits of information in return. After
the second time Mr. Krahal's aid proved helpful to the crew, they
came to him for information and he was happy to help. Consulting
my elements of patronage above and seeing that Mr. Krahal was
a very powerful patron and also had a strict and alien ideology, I
offered the players a deal: exactly the information they needed,
obtained supernaturally and with unerring accuracy, in exchange

for stealing a certain codex from a holy place he could not enter. They agreed, and the official patronage relationship was established.

While Mr. Krahal was very active in the story, and in fact eventually succeeded in his goal (more or less ending our game in a bizarre blaze of glory), he was always only reactive. The players released him, so he helped them in return. They had goals aligned with his, so he helped them. They needed money, so he supplied it, requiring only their help in return. At every step, Mr. Krahal was working toward his long-term goal and the short-term goals that constituted it, but he was doing so in response to the player's actions. Ultimately, it was the players' actions that led to Mr. Krahal's ultimate attainment of his goal: Without their help, he would never have been able to release his master from the chains under the city.

Mr. Krahal was a blast to play and run. He is an example of a very powerful, high-level patron pursuing goals that are contrary to the player characters' goals (in this case, living and breathing), but more than willing to provide assistance and resources as they require. The small favors he required of them were his way of working toward his short-term goals, but the players were never aware of his long-term goal. That plot thread was there for them to pull on, if they desired, but they didn't. The world changed in response to their actions. Just not in a good way. —*JF*

Chapter 4

──❦·❧──

LOCATIONS

S O FAR IN THIS BOOK, we've talked a lot about drama and action. In our proactive fantasy games, we rely on character motivations and faction goals to create tension and drive the story forward. When the tension becomes too great to contain through roleplay, we break out the dice.

But there is a consequence to this approach: The characters need a reason to fight. Even if that fight isn't actual armed combat, characters need a reason to pursue their goals. This character motivation can take many forms, and as Game Masters, we know we often need to motivate the players as well as their characters. Many of the other elements we'll discuss are motivations: how to make your players and your characters care about the things they're doing and how to work together to creatively find more things to do in your game world. We'll tackle locations first.

Locations as Motivations

Locations are far more than backdrops in your story. Instead of thinking of them simply as "your settings," consider locations as plot devices. Though most cannot drive your story forward on their own, the way characters feel about a tavern, a town or a tower of learning certainly can. A strong emotional connection to a location can serve as a foundation for that character's goal. The stronger the emotion a character feels about a place, the stronger the goal. As the Game Master, you can help your characters form emotional attachments to the game's locations and give them both motivation for pursuing their goals and places to create goals around.

For example, consider the archetypal small frontier town that many adventurers find themselves wandering through at some point during a fantasy RPG. If the characters are passing through when an orc horde attacks the town, they may or may not fight to defend it. Game Masters often assume our players will have the same emotional connection to the non-player characters and locations as we do. This is rarely the case.

In fact, I've had player characters join in and aid the rampaging orcs and do a little looting of their own. But if the characters have a prior emotional connection to the town, they may have a reason to fight. If a family member or an ally who is a skilled craftsman lives there, for example, the character might fight to defend their home or business. On the other hand, if the townspeople were rude or aggressive and the characters have a negative emotional connection to the place, the orc attack is an opportunity to play out some interesting character choices—revenge, schadenfreude or a chance to turn the tables. Characters invested (one way or the other) in this town might create short-term goals like "protect the town from the orc invasion" or "help the orcs raze the town."

These emotional connections don't have to be attached to NPCs, either. Consider the extensive realm beneath the surface, the tight, twisting maze of caverns underneath the surface of the earth, a realm unto itself. If you give the player characters a reason to fear and hate the dark, their motivations involving that region will be much stronger for it. Perhaps they need to venture through the Underdark to find a certain person or item. Instead of just a skill check to be passed, the location of the Underdark could pose a real, plot-based danger they want to avoid or present a problem to be solved—both are foundations for a strong PC goal.

BACKWARD LOCATION DESIGN

In order to make locations memorable and emotionally charged, don't come up with a cool idea and then attach a quest to it later. This may lead to mechanically interesting combat and exploration, but it won't lead to emotionally invested players. Instead, work backward; that is, analyze player goals to figure out what a satisfying conclusion to their efforts will be and design a dungeon crawl, castle siege or tower defense around that idea.

You can still use all the dungeon designs and encounter tables you've been prepping, but they should all be working inside the framework of pursuing that PC goal. The end result is a location that is memorable, emotionally significant and mechanically satisfying—a location with a body crafted around its soul, rather than a soul stuffed into an already-existing body.

This backward design is much easier than it sounds. If you have a clear idea of your PC and faction goals, it's almost trivial. If you don't, or if they change often, then collecting that information is actually harder than the dungeon design. Once you have them, though, you should run through the following questions for each goal, then read through each of the sub-sections below with your answers in mind.

1. Is this goal already tied to a location?

If a character's goal is already tied to a location, that location is one you'll need to design for. If it's not a very interesting or exciting location, think of ways you could make it more interesting or raise the stakes (see Chapter 5).

Examples: Destroy the One Ring in the fires of Mount Doom, free Flynn Rider from his prison cell, enter the lost city of Rhuidean.

2. If this goal is not tied to a location, what sort of location would present a chance for a character to accomplish it (or die trying)?

Most goals will end in conflict, with the winner achieving their goal and the loser failing theirs, or vice versa. In what place will this conflict likely happen? Try to think of an interesting location where this goal could be completed in order to send your players or your factions there.

Examples: Find the six-fingered man who killed my father (location: the feast hall in the well-armed six-fingered man's castle), discover the identity of the Dragon Reborn (location: the town square during a holiday festival in the small town where the Dragon Reborn might be living), find a burglar to recruit to your party's dangerous mission (location: the hobbit-hole of a certain burglar recommended by the party wizard).

3. In pursuit of which goal was this location created?

Some person or faction might have created the place of interest in which your players find themselves, so consider why it was built. This will give you an idea of exactly where it will be, what it will look like and so on. Form follows function: If you know why your location is a certain way, you will be able to design what it looks and feels like.

Example: The sky cells in the Eyrie hold high-risk prisoners, so they need to be well-lit, have very few entrances and exits and be easily observable by jailors. They're used for punishment as well as containment, so they have one wall open to mountain air and a drop that means certain death: psychological torture for the imprisoned.

4. Which factions have a presence in this location, and what forces stand in the PC's way? As the character seeks the completion of their goal, what forces stand against them? If a faction has a presence in that location, they might oppose the players. If the faction controlling your location is friendly, maybe a different faction is moving toward the location at the same time as the players and will offer resistance. Though most conflicts in this genre are armed and dangerous ones, this rule applies to social and stealth encounters, too. If nothing stands in the character's way, there is no drama. Who or what opposes them? Natural forces? Devious mechanisms created by long-dead architects? A lack of shared language? Think explicitly about who and what will oppose the character in their pursuit of their goal.

Examples: Ancient dungeons are guarded by the still-ticking steam mechanisms of their genius designers, the twisting paths inside the dragon's dream are guarded by sentient enchantments, the Eye of the World is guarded by two of the Forsaken.

There are many ways to encourage your player characters to form emotional connections with the locations in your game. The type and strength of the connection will depend on what kind of place it is and the role it plays in your game. We've outlined a few categories you will likely include in your game below. In each section, we discuss the role of the location type in your game and how you can get your players to form emotional connections with these places that will inform their goal-driven play.

Player Bases

A character's base is a staple of many TTRPGs. Once a group accrues enough wealth, power and influence, a base is the perfect way to display it. It can allow them to defend themselves, stake political power, gain followers and, most importantly, give them something they care about. This can be a powerful tool for storytelling and plot hooks and gives more opportunities to build goals around and work toward, whether by players or NPCs.

Bases are a place for players to gather, plan, store their loot, house allies, build and design things, research, collect, hold their enemies and a thousand other functions. Examples of bases include the Batcave, Kholin's Warcamp and Rivendell. Each serves as a place to gather, plan, fortify and recuperate between adventures.

ACQUIRING A BASE

Bases are themselves a boon to our games, as the mere act of having one is a goal in itself. Building a base, hiring workers for it and, most of all, maintaining it are goals that require and encourage player proactivity.

To obtain a base, players generally need to go through some sort of trial and tribulation. Bases are generally either built specifically by the players or granted as a reward. Rewards are for a later chapter, so for now let's limit ourselves to building bases (although rewarding sturdy land or ruins that make it easier for characters to build bases certainly won't hurt your gameplay).

Players will first need to determine the function of their base and spend money to get it built. Nickels and dimes are a distraction here— they don't need to know any specifics of building the base, especially if they don't want to. The amount of cash and how long it takes to build are really all that's important, and the party can keep running around on adventures in the meantime. Obtaining the base is a goal in and of itself, making money more of an objective than a value to build up to, if applicable at all (the end result of "earn enough money for a base" and "capture the local fort" is the same: finding a place to call home).

With these concepts in mind, we can adjust our plan accordingly. Using the base-building tools outlined above, approach it step by step:

1. If the players are building a base to fulfill a specific goal, tie the location to it closely (build a keep to hold the narrow pass).

2. If the goal of the base is linked to a specific location, ensure the players can build there (build a mighty forge in the heart of a volcano).

3. How does the goal behind the base's creation affect its appearance, structure, layout and furniture/equipment? (A base in which to research spells will likely have a large stone tower filled to the brim with libraries, books and strange spellcasting components.)

4. What factions are present in the area? Did the players call on their allies for aid when building or defending the base? (The party has issues during construction and calls on the thieves guild for some ill-gotten coin to finish the project. As a result, the guild is now allowed to operate some gambling dens in the small town.)

USEFUL BASES AND BASES AS GOALS

Bases should have a use of some kind. A castle can be a great method of defense, while a lodge in the woods may be more useful as a hiding place for when your characters inevitably get into trouble. Giving bases a specific function can also be a great way to reward players—a blacksmith's forge, a secret exit or traps—these are all ways to grant tangible benefits to a group for the trouble they have to go through to get a base in the first place.

This kind of reward has the built-in benefit of the base serving as a tool for completing goals: A surprising number can be completed or assisted with a base. Defensive- and community-oriented goals, for example, nearly always benefit from running a stronghold or castle of some kind, and if the base's use is maintained, it serves as a conduit for players to complete longer-term goals.

Using a base in a story hook or goal is also an easy way to encourage player engagement. After the blood, sweat and tears they had to provide in order to gain one, many players get emotionally attached to their base. Therefore, when some evil undead mage-king they've angered comes to collect his due, the group may fight tooth and nail to protect it.

Be careful not to overuse this goal. If the players are constantly stuck returning home to defend their base, it quickly becomes less of an advantage and more of a chore and distraction. Spacing out attacks and making them more dire threats grants tension and drama to the battle. Should the characters lose? Perhaps they need to plan a daring return to reclaim what's rightfully theirs.

MAPPING A PLAYER BASE

In more tactical, combat-driven games, it will inevitably become necessary to create a map. Doing so is a huge opportunity for player agency; let your players make it. Less work for you, great fun for them. Of course, if your players don't want to bother, sure, draw one up, but in my experience, players jump at the opportunity to make something "real" in the game and will typically work much harder to defend a self-designed base. It gets even better when presented as a battle map, complete with traps they set a la *Home Alone*—this is their turf, and anyone who intrudes will pay the price.

Allowing players to make the bases on a more minute scale allows them to create new subgoals that further a "protect my home" goal. "Secure guards," "manufacture a powerful arcane trap" or "create a front entrance made of magical metal" present a few fun short-term goals tied to the larger aim of better securing the area.

Cities and Settlements

In most TTRPGs, "going back to town" means taking time to rest, heal, shop and possibly look for work. Town, no matter the size, is a change of pace from adventure, which usually takes place outside the safe confines of the town (especially if we count the ever-popular sewers under a town as being outside the town). The change of pace of returning to everyday life is an important part of the game since it provides a different style of play and a good time for players to stretch their real legs and grab a snack. Examples of these in traditional fantasy include Castle Black and Tar Valon, both of which served as a place for the party to resupply, heal and focus on other goals.

In fantasy roleplaying games, "town" is often skimmed over or forgotten in terms of its potential as an interesting, engaging location on its own terms. Players have the tendency to treat the town as a fuel stop, replenishing their stocks of potions and projectiles before setting off again toward the "real" game. But in a proactive fantasy game, the NPCs and factions that populate the towns are an important part of the world. This makes cities and settlements convenient hooks for players to emotionally invest in and design goals around. The rest and aid they receive in town (such as a bard with a lovely voice, an old flame who still lives in the character's former neighborhood or a kindly elderly man who tells their fortune for free) provide reasons to care about the location. Keeping track of the important parts doesn't need to be complicated, and it will strengthen your players' connection to the world while providing you with more interesting people, places and events to build your game on.

There are many things that make up a city or a settlement in a fantasy game, but we will focus on just three of them: people, resources and change. These three factors contribute the most to making a city feel important and alive. They are also the factors your players will care the most about, which means these are the factors players will form goals around.

PEOPLE LIVING IN CITIES AND SETTLEMENTS

The defining feature of a city or a settlement is that it is where many people come together for trade, education, religious devotion and more. This can make the Game Master's job difficult, as we often feel we need to keep track of many people in a city and remember who they are, what they want, their history with the characters, etc: Does the new mayor like the adventuring party? What about the mayor's son? How does the town alchemist feel about the party cleric's sermons?

This type of individual tracking is unnecessary. One of the reasons to run a proactive game is to save time and effort since the story develops naturally from the actions of the players. This same principle applies to the people living in cities and settlements: it's more convenient for us to organize our settlement around major factions instead of the individual members in them. If the players are interested in a particular faction or NPC important to it, you'll know and can design them when needed, instead of filling in all the details ahead of time. Just decide which factions (and which NPCs affiliated with them) are active in your city or settlement and you'll have a built-in reason for the party to care, since you already designed factions and NPCs with goals that interact with the players.

This simplifies our bookkeeping a great deal, since we don't need to keep track of every merchant—just the merchant's guild; we don't need to track every single senator—just the Senate; we don't need to know every senior adventurer's position on an issue—just the position of the Adventurer's Guild. There are situations in which infighting and a difference of opinion in factions is interesting and appropriate, but it's less often than most Game Masters think.

Sure, it is realistic for everyone in an organization to have slightly different goals and for some of them to be at odds with one another—but that doesn't mean the organization itself is unclear about the goals it is slowly and inexorably moving towards. These goals are the ones that should intersect with player goals, sparking conflict and catalyzing adventure.

Therefore, an important part of your city or settlement design should be considering who lives there, what they want and how they are likely to go about getting it (the groundwork laid in Chapter 3 is essential for this). You can invent names of specific NPCs as needed and place them into factions as you see fit. That way whenever you need a new character, you aren't pressed to make them up on the spot—you can simply decide which faction(s) they are affiliated with, assume goal alignment with that faction by default and then make any necessary changes later.

Besides being easier for you to track, this approach has the added benefit of keeping your game focused on the major conflicts you've already put in place, which is good for keeping players engaged. If you have a few important NPCs, you can flesh those out separately— but I think you will find yourself doing this less frequently once you see the flexibility and utility of a factions-first approach.

Finally, even though we should plan our settlements ahead of time to be of significance to the players, it doesn't always work out that way. Sometimes the players visit someplace we want them to have a connection to, or we want to strengthen their connection to an existing location. If you're having trouble figuring out how to do this by relating the people in your settlement to your group's PC goals, try rolling on the table below.

1d8	Connection to PC Goal
1	Person of interest to PC goal was last sighted here.
2	A faction hostile to the group is headquartered here.
3	A faction allied with the group is headquartered here.
4	A powerful local faction shares a player's goal.
5	A PC owes a favor to a faction active here.
6	A faction active here owes a favor to a PC.
7	A new faction has formed here in direct opposition to a PC goal.
8	A new faction has formed here in direct support of a PC goal.

GOAL-RELATED RESOURCES AVAILABLE IN CITIES AND SETTLEMENTS

As mentioned, one big draw for characters visiting town is the promise of what can be acquired there. In most TTRPGs, "town" means repairing weapons, replenishing potion stocks and healing up. In some games, it means hiring a diviner, enchanter or guide.

These resources go a long way toward making players feel invested in a particular location. Every Game Master knows that one surefire way to get players interested in something is to attach a consistent source of loot to it, so we can exploit this in our city and settlement design to make our locations instantly important to our players. Best of all, PC goals that involve getting more or better stuff can be attached to these locations and give the players a reason to care about them.

Recall when the exhausted party from *The Hobbit* reaches Rivendell for the first time. They eat fine elven food, rest and recover in a serene grove and even gain some useful information and items to aid them in their quest. As a result, Bilbo Baggins forms such an emotional attachment to Rivendell that he not only writes of it with extreme fondness but actually retires there instead of staying in his ancestral home in Bag End! The resources and vibes that Rivendell contains and represents made it feel like home to Bilbo, even more so than the Shire, where he spent most of his life.

When creating your city or settlement, you'll need to decide what resources are available there and how the characters will be able to access them. As you make those choices, you'll not only be deciding how significant this city or settlement will be to your players, but also conveying your setting's tone and this location's culture and atmosphere. In some cases, you might also consider which resources are not available in a given settlement (most settlements have a pool of standard resources available—replacement weapons within reason, ammunition, beds, food and drink—but it is sometimes interesting to take one or more of those away if it fits the setting of your current adventure).

To attach object- or resource-related player goals to a settlement, first consider what the players might be able to get their hands on there. If you like maps, consider the geography of the place–is there a particular natural resource close by, like rare metal ores or timber? Are they on a mountain, cliff or hill? Are they near a trade route that might provide access to luxuries? Are they near a magical anomaly that might provide magical items? Is it a religious, cultural or enchanted site?

To make your city or settlement stand out, try to pick one resource it is known for that is harder or more expensive to get anywhere else. This lends some local flavor to the town, helps players remember it and allows you to get creative with your worldbuilding. In larger cities, there might be room for more than one good or service.

Once you know which resources the players will be able to access, you can attach a player goal to your settlement. The key here is to make the stuff available in this town the means of pursuing an important goal, not the goal itself: it's not that the town has magic swords lying around, it's that the town is known for skilled blacksmiths and a supply of magical crystal ore. The players can pursue or leverage these resources however they want, which will inform the next arc of your game.

Notice we aren't tailoring the resources of the settlement exactly to the players' needs. Don't choose a goal first and decide on the resources later, unless there's no other option—this doesn't feel natural, and if every town the players encounter happens to have the exact solution to the problem they're currently working on sitting in a mine or at the bottom of a lake nearby, it feels like the world revolves around them. Instead of settling for this kind of too-convenient pattern, look at the full list of player goals and connect your city or settlement to the one that matches best. This keeps goals from being forgotten, gives everyone some time in the spotlight and makes the world feel much more natural.

If you're having trouble connecting your city or settlement to your player goals, consider consulting the table below. You can roll 1d8 or choose an entry that corresponds to a resource available in a city or settlement.

1d8	Local Resource a City or Settlement Is Known For	Related Player Goals
1	Nearby magical anomaly with a unique effect.	Cure an illness or curse, empower or repair a magic item, locate an important magical crafting component.
2	Natural resources of a rare or very fine quality (wood, ore, stone, etc).	Construct a building or base, repair a damaged location, secure a trade deal.
3	Unusual or rare wildlife in or around the town.	Obtain a rare crafting ingredient, prove the existence of a magical creature, commune with a particular nature deity.
4	Site(s) that store holy or cultural artifacts of great importance.	Gain favor with a god, complete a pilgrimage, connect with their heritage.
5	Source of rare or unique magical ingredients.	Invent a new magical device, complete a difficult crafting process, learn or invent a new spell.
6	Local vegetation of great culinary or alchemical value.	Learn or discover a recipe, obtain a rare and expensive gift, progress a magical or alchemical study.
7	Awe-inspiring natural or geological features.	Defend a sacred natural place, gain the favor of a natural god or powerful woodland creature, overcome a personal trauma.
8	Production facilities capable of making certain items at the highest quality.	Craft a powerful item, learn a crafting discipline or trade, recruit a skilled craftsman.

Once you know what goodies are available in this location, think about how the characters can access them. Most Game Masters stick to a traditional hard currency system (so many gold pieces for so many goods), but that option can limit the party and your creativity. There are many other ways to secure resources: alternative currencies, bartering, favor trading, rare commodities trading, debt accumulation, secret trading, questing, etc. Don't limit yourself to prices in gold pieces when these other options exist. They allow you to attach plot hooks to certain resources while conveying information about what the locals place importance on. For example, if your party recently encountered a dangerous beast in the wild and were forward-thinking enough to keep its horn, such an item might be worth a favor to the right city-dweller.

We don't usually lean entirely into a barter economy or information-based economy, mostly because of the bookkeeping involved. Most necessities and small purchases can be made with cash, hand-waved away or relegated to a "wealth" roll. But for the important goods, or ones we want players to work for, we will break out the alternative economies or require characters to complete certain goals in order to obtain them.

Consider an enchanter who needs a certain magical tool to work and who tells the characters where it might be found or a bookie who needs protection at an upcoming event. These types of plot hooks serve the dual purpose of getting the players invested in a location and providing them with goods or services they would otherwise not have access to.

CHANGING CITIES AND SETTLEMENTS

Cities and settlements are filled with people and factions pursuing power, control, resources and other goals—even the sleepiest little backwater town has these kinds of conflicts on a small scale. In a proactive game, the player characters are relentlessly pursuing their goals in a way that affects the world around them. That means the political, social and economic landscapes of these cities and settlements are always changing.

In our experience, this is the secret sauce that makes the world feel alive. When the game world changes around our PCs and they are directly responsible for that transformation, they feel powerful and invested in the world. When the game world changes around our PCs and they're not directly responsible for those changes, it communicates that the world is vast and exists outside of their adventures. We want to create both of these types of change in every city and settlement. As a rule of thumb, try to have at least one element of every city or settlement change every new time the players visit, with changes becoming more dramatic the longer the players have been away.

The first type of change, player-caused change, is the most straightforward one. When the players complete a goal, simply consider how that goal's completion might affect this city or settlement, if at all. If the player's goal is to warn the town of an impending attack, the change is obvious: barricades, more guards, etc. But if the player's goal is to become a master blacksmith, perhaps the town can change in a few interesting ways. We might have hopeful apprentice smiths appear in the town looking for a mentor, or even an established smith advertising to compete with the player. You might even have certain prominent individuals wearing objects crafted by the player as a status symbol. Sometimes, as in this last example, the changes we've engendered have no immediate effect on the plot but contribute a great deal to the players' conception of having changed the world in some measurable way.

More commonly, players will not be the main instigators of change in the cities and settlements they visit. Instead, change comes from a faction (very common) or an NPC (uncommon). When a faction with a presence in the city achieves a goal, consider how that changes the city. Did the merchant's guild succeed in running competitors out of business? Then there should be boarded-up shops and higher prices. Did the town council approve a public works project? Then you need construction going on somewhere prominent, and perhaps a pack of animals or monsters disturbed by the construction. Did a band of nomadic people get permission to stay inside the walls? Consider having tents or wagons serve as a pop-up district where exotic goods or services might be found.

These are just a few examples of how simple faction goals can dramatically change a city or settlement. More ambitious or destructive goals could cause even greater or more permanent changes. Once you have fleshed out your factions, you may have the opportunity for many instances of change at once, and that's a good thing! This picks up the pace and contributes to the feeling of dynamic change in the world. The key is to never have the characters return to town to find nothing

NPCs AS RESOURCES

When I know a city has certain resources that the party wants, I prefer to use NPCs as a conduit to get the resources from the pool to the players. Patrons, shopkeeps, allies—all of these are easy ways to directly say "There are these things available, here's how you get them" without breaking the immersion of your game. It's also an easy gateway to bargaining, if that's what your players enjoy. —TF has changed at all. No matter how low the stakes or how small or sleepy the town, there is always someone who wants something and will change the current state of things to get it.

Wilderness

The wilderness is, in my experience, by far the most overlooked aspect of location. In a typical campaign, every area an adventurer explores is defined by the people who inhabit it and what they've built there—the town, the dungeon, the lair. The wilderness is usually an afterthought, used for some quick description as they move through it. Possibly, there's some random encounter thrown in, completely detached from the actual events of the story, in which a wild bear shows up, a few dice are rolled and the party ventures forward as though nothing happened.

That type of wilderness is unbelievably boring. A traditional fantasy campaign is defined by the wilderness, and the untamed wild has provided some of the most memorable encounters in campaigns we've played. The wilderness is a key aspect of many games, and transforming it from a slog to an adventure can completely change the tone of a campaign for the better. When applying wilderness to a proactive game, we can use it in two ways that differ from the norm. The first is to simply attach goals to the wilderness itself, allowing players to pursue them in the wilds. The other is to use the wilderness as a challenging conduit to player goals, a built-in aspect of the quest to complete the goal by placing needs or wants on the opposite side of the wilderness or right smack dab in the middle.

Not every campaign needs the wilderness. For example, two of our favorite campaigns, one as a GM and one as a player, in two separate game systems, took place entirely in a single city. We spent months and years of play without ever stepping foot outside the city walls. That said, many of the concepts presented in this chapter don't necessarily have to be used in the "grass and trees" wilderness. These concepts can be applied to many different scenarios. We've applied them to urban campaigns in 5e, a traditionally wilderness-heavy TTRPG through applying typical aspects of "wilderness" (unknown areas, exploration, and the like) and reflavoring them with an urban theme.

While examples of the wilds can be found in the real world, they can take very different forms and present different challenges in fantasy. The Old Forest is very different from the blasted landscape of Mordor; the wilds outside the Two Rivers are very different from the Blight. In each case, the way that wilderness is designed presented challenges and opportunities for the protagonists that directly related to the goals they were pursuing.

THE THEORY OF WILDERNESS

We firmly believe wilderness can be an essential facet of any TTRPG. Whether it's the woods beyond the village, the rough end of town or the harsh reaches of outer space, wilderness represents something important to any game: the unknown. The forest beyond the city is more than a place where goblins live—it's where a goblin fortress is located, and where the players must venture if they are to gain loot and stop the goblin raids. Wilderness as a concept is primarily the land outside the city, but the same ideas can be applied to the surrounding slums outside the tavern. It is a beyond what would usually be considered safe, which means it's dangerous by default. And, more often than not in our games, danger = adventure.

One of the most important facets of the wild is its impact on characters. Many prominent games have "Law" and "Chaos" in their alignment systems. In older editions of those games, and at many tables

Lasting Resolve

In a recent 13th Age game I ran, my level 1 players started in the frontier settlement of Lasting Resolve, a coastal town used as a staging port for explorers and traders on a new continent.

Lasting Resolve didn't exist for its own sake. It was the Empire's foothold on a new continent, ripe with resources and people for plundering. The current denizens of the continent were fighting tooth and nail to keep the Empire out, and the Empire was months away by ship, too distant to respond quickly to any attacks. This meant that Lasting Resolve was a fort, a place for the Empire to keep its tenuous hold on the coast while planning to build larger fortified settlements inland.

This told me the people living in Lasting Resolve weren't farmers or shepherds, like those in other towns of this size in the area. It was a town of soldiers, mercenaries, cutthroats and merchants. These were people looking to make a quick buck. I had the representatives of the Empire, who exerted a hierarchical military-like control over the town, a few mercenary companies and a merchant's guild. Also interested in the town but with very few representatives were a druid's circle and a holy order, both tasked with defending against imperial invaders. I only had two names picked out for people involved in all these factions—I knew what the organizations wanted and how they would pursue it, so I didn't need specific characters.

Given its importance as a frontier foothold for the Empire, Lasting Resolve was always changing. As the players scouted more of the wilderness and clashed with local orcs, the town was fortified and refortified based on their actions and advice. Ships arrived with more weapons and soldiers based on the efforts of local factions, and the town was even flooded after a bad storm caused by an enemy faction's weather-changing ritual. But when the orc tribe faction whose goal was "raze the town of Lasting Resolve" succeeded in just a few rolls and none of the local factions or the PCs were in a position to stop them, I simply wiped Lasting Resolve off the map. The players with goals concerning the orc horde were forced to retreat and regroup, furiously formulating new goals and vowing their revenge. The PCs' connection to Lasting Resolve and their related goals turned it into a living part of the world—and eventually a dying part, too. —*JF* today, that struggle was represented by the civilized world and the wilds. For nature-oriented characters, forests, swamps and a distinct lack of roads don't signal a dangerous encounter—they're a lifeline to their most deeply held beliefs about humanity's place in the universe. On a smaller and more exciting scale, they're a great opportunity for short-term goals such as "eliminate the loggers razing my forest," "halt the production of roads and therefore the spread of civilization" and "plant a grove of sacred trees and keep them from being chopped down." Use these characteristics to build goals for characters and connect them more profoundly to tangible aspects of the wilderness.

THE ENCOUNTER IN THE WILD

The area where many GMs begin to find issue is in planning an actual encounter in the wilderness. We've found this is because many GMs are still stuck in the mindset of the dungeon encounter cycle: monsters attack a village, then the players go and beat them up in neat little dungeon corridors, presented in their own rooms. This is a lovely part of the game, and there's absolutely nothing wrong with using it. But problems arise when this is the only technique GMs employ. The most open-ended dungeon is still a dungeon, and encounters are chained together in ways the GM studies and memorizes. When the rooms and hallways disappear, GMs begin to flounder about in the trees trying to replicate the magic of their tried and true formula and adventure becomes harder to conjure.

The encounter—not the adventure (or dungeon)—should be the essential building block of your game. With this in mind, you can expand your horizons, filling your wilderness with adventure by designing encounters based on players goals instead of random monster tables.

A QUICK ASIDE ON ENCOUNTERS AS THE FUNDAMENTAL UNIT OF PLAY

You'll notice we keep talking about "encounter design" in these chapters, and we rarely mention "adventure design" or even "adventures" at all. This is because when you're encouraging players to be proactive, they are the source of the adventures for the table. The goals they choose to pursue naturally lead to longer plots as the goals run together and influence each other. As the facilitator of the fun, you respond to the players' choices by introducing new plot ideas and organizing the changes in the world, which the players then respond to by formulating new goals, and you continue to bounce off each other in a beautiful, if chaotic, dialectic of fun.

In our proactive fantasy game design philosophy, we consider the encounter to be the fundamental unit of design. When a player announces which of their character goals they'd like to pursue, we don't need to plan an adventure around it—the adventure has already been outlined ahead of time because the goal has been created.

Instead, we turn our creative attention to the obstacles that might be in their way, the specific encounters that will facilitate the conflict. The goal itself often makes the nature of these encounters quite clear—perhaps hordes of orcs, dangerous traps or devious nobles are obstructing them.

We can design encounters as self-contained obstacles to the character goal and arrange them in a web around the object. As the players navigate the encounters, solve or unlock the puzzles or kill the NPCs involved, they get closer to the goal.

We don't need to design traditional adventures because we design our encounters around the player's goals. This organization is connected by the common plot threads of the character goal and becomes an "adventure" in hindsight—but it's one we discover through the process of play, rather than planning it out beforehand. —JF

ADVENTURING IN THE WILD

Aimlessly wandering in the wilderness isn't very fun (in most cases). The wilds are about exploration—they're the journey, not the destination. In the dungeon mindset, wilderness usually devolves into a string of random encounters with wild animals. But we want our players to be the active force, and the world to respond to them instead of the other way around. How can we approach this when they're just rolling a few Wisdom (Survival) checks to get from Point A to Point B?

If you want your wilderness to be an important part of your proactive fantasy game, you either need to attach goals to the wilderness itself or present the wilderness as an obstacle to pursuing the goal. Consider two of our examples from earlier, both from Robert Jordan: the wilderness outside the Two Rivers and the Blight north of the Borderlands.

In *The Eye of the World*, the group from Emond's Field wants to escape from Trolloc pursuit, and they use their knowledge of the relative wilderness to do this: They flee through the trees, hide in hollows and groves and eventually use the river to cut off pursuit, which they achieve using the wilderness itself.

Consider tying some of your player's goals to the wilderness itself in the same way, rather than a dungeon within the wilderness. The terrain, hostility or resources of the wilderness might be just what they need to complete a goal. For inspiration, consider the following table. Find a goal on the left that best matches one of your players' goals, then read across the row to see how it might be adapted to a wilderness setting.

Player Goal	Adapted Wilderness Goal
Learn a powerful spell.	Learn a powerful spell from a forest spirit said to inhabit a wilderness area.
Obtain rare ingredients for a project.	Obtain rare ingredients that cannot be cultivated and must be foraged in the wild.
Escape pursuit.	Use natural terrain features to confuse and evade pursuers.
Slay a powerful beast.	Disrupt a natural ecosystem to lure a powerful beast out of hiding.
Locate a missing person.	Locate a person trapped on a boat traveling down a swift river.
Prove devotion to a god.	Defend a sacred forest from encroaching loggers or poachers.

Later in *The Eye of the World*, certain characters must travel north into the Blight, a vast rotting expanse of hostile wilderness, to locate an important structure (that we might call a dungeon). In this situation, the wilderness itself is the obstacle to the goal the group is pursuing. Poisonous plants, dangerous wildlife and roving bands of enemies made that trek dangerous. The fact that the Eye was out in the Blight, totally inaccessible to the characters, was essential to the difficulty of the challenge before them.

If you'd like more of a wilderness theme to your adventures, consider which goals might have a wilderness encounter as a natural obstacle. Instead of tacking on a wilderness encounter to an unrelated goal, identify goals for which wilderness encounters are a logical obstacle. If you're having trouble thinking of goals to obstruct with wilderness encounters, consult the table below. Find a player goal on the left that matches or is similar to one in your game, then read across the row to see how you might attach it to a location or faction that would make a wilderness goal a natural obstacle.

Player Goal	Adapted Wilderness Goal
Get revenge on a criminal.	Get revenge on a criminal who has fled society and lives in the wilds as an outlaw.
Protect a merchant's investment.	Escort a merchant's goods through a dangerous wilderness area.
Locate a powerful magic item.	Recover a powerful magical item from a ruined location that has been swallowed by wilderness and whose very location is unknown.
Interpret an important prophecy.	Obtain star chart information needed for interpreting a prophecy from a circle of standing stones in the deep wilderness.
Recruit a powerful faction.	Gain the trust of a faction that dwells in the far reaches of an inhospitable place.
Prove devotion to a god.	Complete a survival trial in a wilderness area holy to a certain god to prove devotion.

Running wilderness encounters can be mechanically difficult, since you don't have all the same tools as you do for a dungeon encounter and the encounters typically take place over larger areas—you have no doors, halls and stone brick to carefully fence your encounter in. But wilderness encounters can be a great way to add variety to your game and to communicate the scope of the world as well as your players' ambitions. Try using the wilderness

One Desperate Sprint

The single best wilderness encounter I have ever run was a chase, a desperate attempt by the players to save their own lives after being betrayed and making some very poor choices. They had released an ancient demon from its prison and began to sprint from it as quickly as they possibly could. This fell into the "conduit" category of wilderness encounters—it was more of a byproduct of other goals, not the focus of them. The players had collectively and organically formed a new short-term goal: "Don't get eaten." The demon had also formed a new goal: "Kill the heroes so no one knows I have returned."

The resulting encounter was a chase: The group fled into the wilds, the winged demon in pursuit. In the darkness, they could see its flaming body in the distance, but the creature carried a long whip it could use to snatch them from afar. They couldn't hope to outrun it, so for nearly an hour and a half, the group made checks for endurance, checks to trick the demon into chasing the sound from a rock they threw and even brief flurries of combat against the unstoppable foe. The faster characters would try to distract it then hide in an effort to find an opportunity to save their companions. Roleplaying, high stake rolls and extremely creative ideas transformed what could potentially be a horrid slog of rolls into a tense and eventful encounter.

What does this encounter in the wilds teach us? For one, the wilderness really wasn't the feature here. An enemy was reacting to the actions of the players, the wilderness was really a background aspect—a condition of the encounter. —*TF*

as a setting for achieving a few goals or attaching a few goals to objectives in the wilderness and see how it goes. You might decide you don't like dungeon crawling so much, after all.

Dungeons and Lairs

The dungeon is perhaps the most iconic setting in our beloved TTRPGs. From sun-baked temple ruins in the badlands to corridors of unholy geometric dimensions deep underground, players know that adventure is only a magically locked (and trapped) door away. From a Game Master's perspective, dungeons are indispensable: They allow us to make full use of the granular close-quarters combat rules that most gaming systems thrive on, provide narrative justification for finding clues and loot and grant full control over the difficulty and tension in our game through controlling the dungeon layout. The dungeon setting is where the world's most popular roleplaying game shines, since dungeon delving is what it was designed to simulate.

Designing the mechanical aspects of dungeons is beyond the scope of this book, and it has been discussed already by many Game Masters smarter and more experienced than us. What we would like to contribute is a discussion of how proactive fantasy games create better dungeons and how to design those dungeons to suit a proactive fantasy game by centering PC goals.

WHAT DO WE MEAN WHEN WE SAY "DUNGEON"?

What is a dungeon? In this context, we mean a location in your game that contains the obstacles your characters must overcome to reach their goals. In typical fantasy games, this is a multi-room, multi-level space with traps, puzzles and monsters. Classics from the genre include *Tomb of Horrors* and *The Temple of Elemental Evil*, but a dungeon might also be a sewer system under a city, a small chapel crypt or a military base. Famous examples from fantasy include Dol Guldur in Mirkwood, Bleak Falls Barrow near Riverwood and the Maze of the Beast in Toran territory.

A dungeon doesn't have to be a series of connected rooms filled with monsters, either. If you think of a dungeon as "the place where conflicts about a specific goal happens," then many things become a dungeon: the one-room tavern the party entered to arrest an infamous bandit can become a small dungeon, and the wind-blasted ruins of an ancient city where the party hides for the night can be a very large dungeon. If you're willing to expand the traditional definition of "dungeon" a little bit, you can design spaces that are meaningful sites of thrilling conflict because they are designed first with player goals in mind.

DESIGNING DUNGEONS FOR INTERESTING CONFLICT

If we think of dungeons as places full of obstacles the players must overcome to achieve their goals, then we know we should design dungeons to be interesting and logical places to put those obstacles. If a player's goal is to rescue a long-lost sibling, then a prison is a fine dungeon to design around that goal. But consider a monster lair full of victims being eaten one by one, or an executioner's block with the sibling being led to their death, or an auction where the sibling is about to be sold into slavery—these are far more interesting locations to attach to the same goal.

If your player characters and factions have chosen good goals that align with their expectations, conflict between these goals will emerge naturally over the course of your game. As you watch this conflict emerge, you can predict where the party will come into conflict with opposing forces, and you can design your dungeons based on those predictions.

In proactive fantasy play, the agency of the players and the desire of their characters is what drives the plot, not the dungeons we design. But the dungeons we design for those goals to be pursued, achieved and failed in are what make the game memorable and exciting. Luckily, we don't need to guess what will make a dungeon encounter significant for players—we already have all the tools we need from our proactive fantasy toolbox.

First, pick a location that makes sense as the site of conflict between the party and whatever stands against them as they pursue a goal. You can also think about a logical place the obstacles they'll have to overcome might be located. For example, a party that wants to extract a family member who has joined a cult will come into conflict with the cult members, so you might choose a secret cult hideout or the cult leader's luxurious mansion as a location to build a dungeon around. If instead your party contains a wizard that wants to learn a spell lost to the ages, the party will need to overcome the obstacles posed by the ravages of time, so you might choose a lost library buried beneath shifting sands or the laboratory of an immortal mage as the location (since those are places where the obstacles the party needs to overcome make sense).

If you're having trouble choosing locations based on goals, consult the table below. Find a PC goal that best matches one at your table, then read across the row about the dungeon locations you might set the object of that goal in. Once you have the location, adapt it for your game using the process outlined in the next section.

DESIGNING THE DUNGEON

Once you have picked a location, ask yourself the backward design questions on pg. 110 to fill in a few more details about your dungeon. After you know more about the space, you're ready to start designing.

Remember that the encounter, not the adventure, is the fundamental unit of play. If you design your whole dungeon expecting characters to take a certain path or explore it in a certain way, you will always be let down. Consider your dungeons a collection of encounters, not a story in itself. The story will emerge organically as characters pursue their goals and attempt to overcome the encounters you've designed.

Use your decisions from the questions on pg. 110 to design some interesting encounters and you won't be disappointed. Approaching dungeon design this way also allows you to intentionally create a balance of different types of encounters, each with its own degree of difficulty. Resist the urge to put "the boss" in the last room. If the characters' goal or the goals of the opposing forces mean throwing the most powerful monster at the party as soon as they step into your dungeon, then that is what should happen! Designing your dungeons as a collection of encounters in an interesting place creates dramatic and unpredictable moments while still ensuring your design is flexible enough to adapt to any strange way the players might approach it.

The encounters you design should be inspired by both the PC goal and the encounter location. Be familiar with the PC goal and the factions and forces that stand in their way, then decide how those factions or forces might appear as encounters in your dungeon. These don't have to be combat encounters, either—how might the purpose for which the dungeon was built pose obstacles to the PC goal? See the next chapter for more detail on how to do this.

If you are having trouble designing dungeons around a difficult PC goal, never be afraid to steal ideas from your favorite media. Think about a book, show or movie in which a character's goal was similar to the one you're thinking about. Where did that goal resolve itself? You might be surprised at what you find.

Anakin Skywalker's goal of "prove myself worthy of Obi-Wan's love" was resolved in a brutal duel on the lava planet of Mustafar. Paul Atreides's goal of "escape the tyranny of destiny" was resolved on the open dunes of Arrakis, far from the throne room he left behind. These are surprising places to find emotional closure, but they work. Don't be afraid to adapt your favorite moments to your gaming table, especially if they don't fit the genre you're playing. You'll have to work harder to make them fit, but the changes you make along the way can be surprising and exciting.

If you're still having trouble, consult the following table. Notice that the obstacles don't all fit neatly into categories of combat, skill or social encounters—it is how your players approach them that will decide how it plays out.

Remember that dungeons aren't just locations. Dungeons can encourage player proactivity when we design them explicitly to be the gauntlets the PCs need to run in order to complete their goals. We do this by thinking about why the dungeons are a suitable location for the completion of the goal and by creating a collection of encounters in direct opposition to those goals.

Player Character Goals	Party Obstacles
Locate a rare or magical object.	A powerful monstrous guardian, a security system, a set of trials or tests.
Slay a particular dangerous person.	Well-trained and well-equipped bodyguards, devious traps, an adoring crowd.
Gain the favor of a local faction.	A saboteur deep in the organization, a rival faction working to undermine the allied faction, local government interference.
Discover the identity of a mysterious person.	A secret society concealing something, a system of ciphers, a confusing prophecy.
Create, repair or improve a powerful artifact.	A difficult-to-work with material, a stubborn craftsman, natural magical interference.
Rescue an important person.	A gang of swashbuckling kidnappers, a moving holding cell, a powerful and hungry monster.
Learn a powerful spell, technique, or secret.	Sages or monks who are distrustful of outsiders, a mad scientist's creations, a gang of novice practitioners.

Player bases, the wilderness, settlements and dungeons are just some of the locations your game might take place in. In most TTRPGs, dungeons are where you'll spend most of your time, so if you're unsure about where the players should go to pursue a certain goal, assume it's a dungeon. Once you have the location and you know which obstacles stand in the party's way, it's time to turn your attention to the most important part of the game: conflict.

Chapter 5

CONFLICT

EPIC BATTLES AND earth-shaking duels are standard fare in fantasy media. Why is it that every book, movie and game ends in a high-stakes fight? We could dismiss this as a feature of the genre writers use out of habit, but there's more to it than that. In fantasy media, everything ends in a fight because the stakes are always set so high and the opposing characters are so committed to completing their goals that coming to blows is often the only way to determine who will prevail. As the villain's intentions come into conflict with the lives of the heroes (or, in proactive fantasy, the other way around!), the tensions start to simmer and tension builds. Neither party can back down, so the opposing forces are left to engage in the last resort of everyone willing to do anything to accomplish their goals : violence.

But not all conflict in fantasy is a fight, and fantasy conflict rarely exists for its own sake. Instead, it arises naturally as a progression of escalating tensions that cannot be resolved any other way. Consider these iconic confrontations at the end of fantasy novels: the Battle of the Black Gate in *The Return of the King* (physical violence) or the Pattern-weaving debate between Rand al'Thor and the Dark One in *A*

Memory of Light (philosophical pugilism). These epic confrontations are the culmination of entire series, events set into motion hundreds of thousands of words earlier. The goals the authors established for their characters at the beginning of the story have finally collided, and the results are spectacular.

Just like in the conclusions of these epic fantasy novels, if the goals your players have chosen for their characters are strong, and the factions and NPCs you place in their way are equally passionate about achieving their own aims, conflict is a given.

That means we can create satisfying conflict by focusing not on the battle itself, but on the stakes the battle represents. There are three things to keep in mind when designing conflicts: the motivation of the player characters, the motivations of the forces opposing them and what winning the conflict means. If you design your encounters (whether they be combat encounters or otherwise) with these three things in mind, every battle will feel like a war worth waging.

How to Start a Fight

Players expect conflict, especially armed conflict, at some point during their adventures. But if the only reason you're fighting is to flex your class features or because the GM says so, the game becomes stale, even for the most seasoned group of hack-n-slash murderhobos. You should not expect players to engage in conflict without a good reason. And there's only so much you can do on your end to get them there.

If your players have unfocused or underdeveloped goals, it might be hard to get them invested in your conflicts. Sometimes, this is an issue you'll need to address directly by helping the player adjust their goals. Other times, you can increase the frequency and value of combat in your games by changing the design of your villains.

In Chapter 3, you created villains as NPCs with goals that were in opposition to player goals. Some of your villains' goals won't necessitate violence, while others will. What you want to avoid is a villain whose goals don't pit them against the party—then they're just potential allies who wear intimidating armor or creepy masks.

If your player wants to protect the wilds near their home, make their enemies clear-cutters and forest arsonists, for example. Whatever you choose, place the characters against the villains where their goals must boil over into confrontation.

If you're having trouble coming up with a villainous goal that is sure to spark conflict with the PCs, consult the table below. Decide why the villain has decided to pursue this goal in context.

PC Goal	Conflicting Goals
Make a holy pilgrimage.	Destroy the pilgrimage site.
Obtain a fabled powerful artifact.	Destroy or obtain the same artifact.
Rescue a loved one from a cult they've joined.	Brainwash that loved one into staying forever.
Take revenge for a wrongful death.	Hide all evidence of the wrongful death.
Establish peace between two factions.	Reignite an ancient conflict between factions.
Restore the honor of a family or faction.	Destroy and supplant a family or faction.
Become renowned at something.	Make that skill completely obsolete.
Earn a tremendous amount of money.	Steal a tremendous amount of earned money.

As you choose goals for the NPCs and factions you're framing as antagonists, consider how you want to balance combat encounters with other types of encounters. If your group likes talking more than fighting, you'll want to introduce villain goals that still overlap with the players' interests, but without being so directly opposed to them that violence is the only solution. If you've set up a zero-sum game, the players will always attack. But if you present a villain whose goals involve the same people, places and objects as the players, but the villain's success doesn't mean the party's total failure, you'll see less combat and more social encounters. This is a great way to add a political angle to your games.

Consider the journey of Frodo, Sam and Gollum in *Return of the King*: All three characters have an interest in the One Ring and conflicting goals surrounding it (Frodo wants to destroy the Ring but sometimes also wants to possess it, Gollum wants to steal it and run away with it and Sam just wants to get rid of the thing and go home). But these goals aren't so diametrically opposed that violence is the only answer. Working together for a time serves all three characters, and the conflict is resolved through stealth and deception, with combat only appearing at the very end of their journey, when Gollum has no other recourse but to bite off Frodo's finger.

If you're having trouble coming up with goals that discourage combat and encourage non-combat encounters, consult the table on the opposite page. The left column has the same categories of common PC goals as the preceding table, but the right column offers less conflict-centric villain goals. Notice how these goals still overlap with the PC goals, but they aren't quite so opposed—there are solutions other than violence here.

PC Goal	Less Conflicting Goals
Make a holy pilgrimage.	Prove the holy site is fraudulent.
Obtain a fabled powerful artifact.	Forge a copy of that artifact for show.
Locate a missing loved one.	Take revenge on that missing loved one.
Take revenge for a wrongful death.	Prove the innocence of the killer.
Establish peace between two factions.	Prolong a conflict between factions for gain.
Restore the honor of a family or faction.	Hide a dark secret of that family's past.
Become renowned at something.	Become more renowned at that thing.
Earn a tremendous amount of money.	Regulate or control the profitable scheme.

CONFLICTS WITH COMBAT

Violence isn't always the answer. But the fantasy genre, especially epic fantasy, has a tendency to settle disputes with battles. Proactive games are no different. What better way to explore your character's willpower than to have them pursue something so fervently they'd be willing to put their life on the line to obtain it? The characters and villains of your world will have many goals they believe in wholeheartedly—we made sure of that in Chapters 1 through 3. As your story unfolds at the table, some goals will be so firmly opposed to NPC or faction goals that violence is the only way they can be resolved.

Consider a player character who wants to plant a tree from her home village on a distant mountaintop. If you followed the design process we've laid out so far in this book, you have assigned a goal in opposition to your player's to an opposing force: an industrious mining guild. The guild's goal might be to secure exclusive mining rights to certain parts of the mountain, with the ability to prosecute trespassers. It could also be something more threatening, like clear-cutting the mountaintop to make transporting minerals from the site easier. These barriers to player goals both serve the greater faction interest, but are directly related to, and in conflict with, the player character's goal.

That said, neither barrier will necessarily lead to violence. The first barrier might necessitate a stealth encounter, and the other might turn into sabotage or a social encounter in which the players convince the mining guild to leave a certain grove alone. Depending on your group,

MOST ENCOUNTERS ARE ABOUT COMBAT

We'll spend less time on non-combat encounters in this chapter than combat encounters. That's because most of the games we play are focused on combat, and because fantasy in general solves its dramatic tension with conflict. Especially in the fantasy work we reference in this book, combat is the preferred way of resolving conflict, since most of the conflict involves "the fate of the known world" and not "where to go to dinner." We are also writing this book with a 5e audience in mind, and the vast majority of that rule set is dedicated to combat. We've chosen to leave all exploration (wilderness traversal; locating people, places and things) and most skill encounters (traps, puzzles) out of this book entirely because those are not built around conflict in the same way combat and social encounters are: They don't represent the dramatic tension that arises between the clash of two or more wills. That said, when a member of your party is close to achieving a goal and is functioning as a perfect, unstoppable force of violence, it's a good idea to throw an obstacle at them that they can't punch their way out of: a dungeon full of traps, a hurricane or an important dinner with their in-laws for which they have to choose the restaurant.

these barriers to their goals might not create enough tension to spark a violent encounter.

Consider instead an opposing faction dedicated to eradicating a certain group of people from the land, including all traces of their memory, for some demonic purpose. That faction has a more specific goal, hunting down and slaying the player character with the plant-a-tree goal and burning the sapling, which they view as the only thing preventing their summoning ritual from transpiring as foretold in the *Tome of Horrors*.

Now that's a goal that will create violent conflict. The faction you've set up in opposition to the player character is committed to a goal in which violence is the only answer. In this scenario, you can be reasonably sure an encounter with this faction will be a violent one, even if the players know it's coming.

The goals you determine for your factions (and the other forces that oppose your players as they strive to get what they want) will influence the frequency and type of combat. If you create a faction of religious zealots hoping to purge the party or create an extremist who has no qualms killing children to please the Hag of Hallifax, you'll get much more combat than if you have factions committed to harmonious alliances or mutually beneficial arrangements. When you design the factions and NPCs that populate your shared world, try to anticipate how their goals will interact with the party's goals. Based on your knowledge of the party, how they prefer to operate and their power level, you can also anticipate which opposing goals will lead to combat.

If you take stock of where things stand and you aren't satisfied with the potential for violence, you can all but guarantee combat encounters in a few ways.

- Strengthening the opposing faction's ideological commitment to their goal (religious or otherwise), making them willing to commit more resources and/or atrocities to ensure they achieve it (including their members' lives).

• Weaken the opposing faction's position relative to rivals—desperate people are more likely to resort to violence.

• Introduce a constraint on the opposing faction's time or resources, making violence a faster (though usually messier) choice.

• Create an NPC belonging to the opposing faction and assigned to pursue the opposing goal who has a personal reason to choose violence, such as a grudge against a PC.

• Have your antagonists shoot first. After all, some men (and women, and devils) just want to watch the world burn.

If these won't work, you may need to revise your opposing faction's goals. Choosing a goal that conflicts more strongly with the party's goals will create more tension, making combat encounters a more likely way to resolve it.

Keep careful track of the goals of your opposing factions to accurately predict when combat is likely to occur. Once you've decided which sets of opposing goals will likely lead to combat, you can begin to design the combat itself with those goals in mind.

GOAL-ORIENTED COMBAT

In most combat encounters, the goal is to defeat the enemy. This is usually a simple matter of hit points and landing enough attacks to take them to zero before the same thing happens to you. But now we have all these lovely character motivations that our players have put thought into and villainous motivations we have crafted in response. What are some things that a fight might be about in addition to hit points? What would it mean to win a fight without one side reducing the other side's hit points to zero?

A straight brawl-type hit point contest is an appropriate combat encounter in some situations, but there's nearly always a better, more engaging option. Consider designing combat encounters around objectives beyond defeating the enemy. This adds variety to your combat and an element of danger not related to defeat, but rather failure: It takes our player character goals, the core of our proactive fantasy game, and injects them directly into the mechanics of our combat encounters. If the party loses the fight, they could lose everything they're fighting for. In a world of resurrection magic, death isn't necessarily the worst thing that can happen to a goal-driven PC. Revivify is not a time machine—once an artifact is stolen or a temple is sundered or a fragile sapling is crushed under the trampling boot of late-stage capitalism, there's no going back.

Consider a party whose goal is to stop a dark ritual from being performed and summoning an ancient evil into the world. We could design combat encounters in a dungeon where the players fight through rooms of cultists, then defeat a summoned demon "boss" in the final room. Or, if we design our combat encounters around objectives instead, we could scrap most of the dungeon and send cultists out into the world to gather certain types of souls in a ritual sacrifice for use in the summoning. Player characters would need to find the cultists and interrupt the ritual in progress to stop the harvesting of souls. This would allow us to set our combat encounters in a variety of locations and possibly tie in other factions and player goals, connecting it to a larger plot. If the players fail to stop enough soul harvests, they might have to enter the dungeon after all to stop the summoning itself. They will meet deadly resistance, but the purpose isn't to kill all the cultists, it's to stop a ritual that is happening during the combat encounter. It allows us to put an alternative win state on the fight (if the ritual is stopped, the cultists will flee, not stand and fight), but more importantly, it allows us to put a different fail state on the fight, since even a party that kills every cultist without taking a scratch might fail to stop the ritual in time. Designing combat encounters around a string of objectives ties the success or failure of the player character goals directly to the success of their actions in combat encounters, which not only aligns the narrative and mechanical aspects of the game but creates synergy between them.

You can design combat encounters around most character goals. Consider a player character who wants to discover the identity of a certain person. Why not corner that person and design a clash around unmasking their identity while they try to escape? Or, if a character wants to obtain a certain object, why not design a fight with a person or monster who has the object and won't give it up without a fight? A player might need to defend a spring of enchanted water from an army of living trees, rescue their beloved sibling from a doppelganger who wants to steal their identity or win a duel blindfolded and with one hand behind their back. Some combat encounters can still turn to slugfests about hit point reduction, but that's not all they have to be. Players will have the option to pursue their goals in an exciting encounter in the way they have the independence to choose—and their choices may surprise you.

The additional objectives you introduce to your combat encounters can be simple or complex but should relate to the goal the fight is about. The ones we most frequently use are:

Defend a location. The fight is won not when all the enemy is dead or defeated, but if whatever you are defending survives the fight. You can introduce a time constraint or enemy reinforcements to increase the stakes.

Capture a location. The fight is won when a location is controlled by the party. You'll need to make the conditions for "control" very clear beforehand. Some locations (an open field) are much harder to "control" than others (a fortified tower), so use the specifics of the location to determine what it means to "control" it.

Destroy an item. The fight is won when a certain object is destroyed (the classic example is an item that allows an enemy to control minions, and destroying the item ends the fight as the minions give up or turn on their master).

Disrupt a process. Stop an enemy from completing a complex process, such as a summoning ritual or operating a siege weapon. Introduce a time constraint (prevent X successes on the enemy's task in Y rounds) to spice things up.

Complete a process. The inverse of the above, where the party must complete a multistep or complex process during a combat encounter. The fight is won when the process is complete. Throw hordes and hordes of weak enemies at the players in these encounters but have them flee or die when the objective is complete—this makes for an epic conclusion to a mid- or long-term goal.

Battle with conditions. The fight introduces some constraints, such as certain weapons being less effective (in tight quarters, only piercing weapons aren't penalized) or murder not permitted (all damage must be non-lethal). If the party fails to meet the condition, you can either declare the fight lost or change the reward in some way.

Covert infiltration. The fight is lost when an alarm is raised and an overwhelming force causes the party to flee. Stealth and engaging only a few enemies at a time is key.

If you're having trouble coming up with additional objectives for combat encounters, consult the table on the next page. Roll 1d8 and check the result on the table, which references a PC goal. Consider how the enemy's goal involves the same people, places or objects and how that determines the additional combat objective. Adjust these ideas to suit your game.

1d8	PC Goal	Enemy Goal	Additional Combat Objective
1	Extract the location of the vampire's coffin from his trusted lieutenant.	Escape scrutiny by traveling by carriage away from danger.	Capture the lieutenant alive.
2	Use the Key of Chaos to enter an ancient vault.	Throw the Key into the lava, forever destroying it.	Obtain the Key before it can be thrown into the lava.
3	Guard the museum's magical urn.	Destroy the urn and scatter the ashes of the dark lord back into the world.	Prevent the object from being damaged or broken.
4	Harness a magical ritual's power to magnify the effects of a spell.	Steal the central component of the ritual to summon a demon.	Complete the ritual without letting attackers into the salt circle.
5	Prevent the salt water from reaching the subterranean slugfolk town.	Flood the caverns and plunder the empty slugfolk town.	Prevent the water level from rising.
6	Humiliate the tyrant king by easily defeating his champion.	Crush the resistance by slaughtering its leaders in gladiatorial combat.	Win the battle without taking a single hit.
7	Kill the corrupt lord without drawing the ire of the other noble.	Prevent the town's rulers from learning of the lord's life of crime.	Slay the noble without being caught or even seen.
8	Ring the correct number of bell chimes to signal an attack from hobgoblin invaders.	Keep the assault force a secret from the enemy town.	Ring the bells in a certain order.

ENEMY TACTICS

Monster tactics are the perfect representation of goals in battle. A goblin will fight very differently than a mighty dragon, and the way monsters communicate, move, improvise and think will vastly change both the tone and stakes of a face-off. Tactics force the players to think more creatively, engage more (and therefore be more interested) and be better combatants. Critical thinking in combat encourages proactive play and keeps the battle tense, allowing for more interesting dynamics between players and GMs.

How can we determine monster tactics? Remember that underlings are an extension of a faction. Enemies and their rulers will have objectives, and as a result of these objectives clashing with the heroes, violence erupts. Observe these goals—how strong are they? Are they worth dying for? Being injured for? How much secrecy do they require? Why someone is fighting also determines how they will behave in battle. A kobold skirmishing over a few chunks of copper will not fight as hard as a knight avenging the death of his true love; one might flee, one might fight recklessly and so on. Extract tactics from the goals of your factions.

How do we apply the goals of a minion's faction? What do these goals represent? Do they carefully align with the battle at hand? An enemy should threaten the players, be involved in a threat to the players or otherwise pose some form of danger in the fight. While considering your combatants, you can think less as a GM and more as an enemy, letting you ease up a little in combat and focus on other things.

Try to enter the headspace of how a given enemy thinks. How does their faction's goals define their own behavior? What beliefs do those groups hold? Do they serve a certain god or code of ethics? Do they dislike members of certain organizations? What values are placed on strength, cunning, bravery, pragmatism? These beliefs can inform certain goals that affect how an enemy behaves in battle. If you're having trouble with this concept or don't have a distinct idea of the faction's goals yet, use the table below to get started.

Faction Goal	Minion Tactic
Create a new code of law in the city.	Never cheat—make sure the opponent doesn't lose due to dirty tactics.
Embody a perfect collective of goals that emphasize group unity.	Attack in groups, never break formation.
Prove a controversial new theorem that redefines magic.	Outwit opponents. Use the terrain, exploit their weaknesses and try to confuse them.
Take back a homeland lost to cowardice long ago.	Never flee, never back down.
Follow the tenets of an ancient warrior-king.	Demonstrate power by challenging the strongest foe.
Take control of the throne.	Backstab allies and make bargains if necessary.
Stay true to the divine tenets of a god, no matter the cost.	Hold true to the tenets of my god, no matter what.
Find redemption in life to be saved from eternal damnation.	Viciously attack any foe that slays an ally.

USING ENEMY TACTICS EFFECTIVELY

In battle, monster tactics can already be partially determined by utilizing their stats and the beliefs of their faction. However, the following guidelines generally make enemies more likely to pose a meaningful threat to the players and force them to think (and react) creatively and proactively:

Clever Enemies Target Certain Foes: Even a stupid beast will target what hurts it most. A clever enemy may target the weaker characters first, as their skill becomes apparent. The truly devious will slay the healer first—no resurrections. This type of tactic only becomes satisfactory when an enemy has researched the players

CASE STUDY

Battle of Pyre Hill

A few years ago, I ran a classic fantasy game that was starting to incorporate some of the elements in this book. We had a large group of players with connections to a faction of druids and rangers tasked with protecting a forest region in the north. When an invading army attacked, the players were called upon for aid and asked to defend a nearby hilltop with a warning beacon. The beacon was an essential part of the communication network in the region, and if the defense failed, it would carry the news south, where the human kingdoms would receive the message and send reinforcements.

The invading army knew the importance of the beacon and sent a small force to take the hill, so the player characters and their hired help went to defend it. The setup of the fight had clear stakes (important information on the outcome of the battle), player motivation (repay a favor to this faction that granted us aid), enemy motivation (greatly increase the odds of successful southern invasion by capturing this information route) and objective (defend the beacon and keep it operational). As it turns out, this combination of factors was a powder keg.

The fight was brutal. It lasted a day and a half (in-game time), and the players refused to give one inch. Faced with overwhelming odds, they did their very best to hold their ground. Their hired help ended up fleeing (their motivation to fight wasn't strong enough to face certain death), but the players managed to keep the invading force at bay. Unwilling to sacrifice more fighters, the enemy withdrew and allowed the players to keep the hill, winning them the combat encounter even though neither side was defeated by losing hit points. Best of all, the fight had lasting consequences: Due to earlier player choices, the main fight at the ranger fortress was lost and the invading army claimed the forest—but news traveled swiftly southward via the beacon system, and armies were mustered to defend the lands. —*JF* and exploits their specific weaknesses. A faction with the goal "prove our intellectual superiority" will use this strategy often.

Use the Terrain: We'll discuss this more in time, but a good enemy needs to know how to use its surroundings. Archers want cover, flying creatures need space to move, a grappler thrives in narrow corridors to avoid being surrounded. Even when out of their element, the enemies will still try to leverage the terrain as best they can. A faction with the goal "defend my home" will likely lean on this strategy.

Work Together: This one, as with every tip, is subject to change given the abilities and beliefs of an enemy, but the majority of foes work best as a team. Just as the balanced dynamic helps keep the party going, a diverse group of enemies keeps players on their toes, especially in a single encounter. A faction with the goal "never lose a warrior" will use this strategy often.

Don't Get Cornered!: Most important of all, lone enemies are often dead meat. When an enemy works with others, they try to surround their opponents, and when alone, they need mobility or else they get pinned down and pulped into hamburger. How do we achieve this? Plan ahead! When a group of enemies rush into battle, they need to plan how they move to get the upper hand in positioning. If a single enemy is fighting for its life, it needs to stay light on its feet, constantly moving out of reach (or be really good at blocking attacks). A faction with the goal "lose as few followers as possible" would use this strategy.

The point of these tactics is to form a connection between the theoretical goals of a faction to the material, concrete actions taken by their members to achieve these goals. By viewing underlings as an extension of factions and tactics as an extension of goals, combat becomes less about a slugfest and more about the objectives that caused it.

CASE STUDY

Boblin the Mighty

In one of my 5e games, a hostile goblin faction wanted to raze a nearby village, with the mid-term goals "burn the town hall to the ground" and "keep the goblin castle secure" and the short-term goals of "take the gates," "slaughter the armed humans" and "get the explosive goblin grog to town hall."

When the players found their old companion, Boblin the Goblin, leading the faction and the villagers, they felt personally betrayed: the fight was on. The faction goals defined Boblin's actions from that moment on: His goal was not to kill the characters. He would, if it was necessary and easy, but that wasn't his main goal. Boblin prioritized protecting the goblin grog and picking off characters that approached the wagon containing it. He also wanted to keep the gates defended, and should they start to fall, he would withdraw and ensure they remained stable to prevent being cornered. Additionally, he needed to destroy the town hall so the players' forces couldn't muster there, so he brought goblin grog with him wherever he went. If the players fled, he wouldn't follow, but if they attacked, he'd defend himself with deadly force. If the players went after the grog or gates, Boblin would target them gleefully.

These tactics were much better than if Boblin had just found the players and fought them. The fight felt like a real clash between opposing forces who genuinely wanted things, instead of a hit point competition. Boblin had his goals, the players had their own and both groups made choices based on the situation for when, where and how to fight. In reactive play, they would have instead stood in an open area, trading blows until one group was reduced to zero hit points. With proactive principles, both the players and Boblin needed to act strategically in order to fulfill their respective goals and thwart their foes. Their choices, made in pursuit of their goals, shaped the fight. —*TF*

Conflicts Without Combat

There are many goals and projects that aren't best solved by violence. Social encounters, skill encounters and roleplaying are all essential parts of the game. The way in which a character decides to pursue a goal and the decisions they make in pursuit of it allow the group to discover that character together, and it's those exciting and surprising decisions that make the game come to life.

Many of the highest-stakes goals aren't achieved through violence at all. One famous example comes at the very end of *The Wheel of Time* when Rand al'Thor confronts the Dark One's champion Ishamael and then the Dark One himself: The part of that conflict that is an actual fight is just a ruse, and the actual conflict takes place over all time and all reality as the highest-stakes debate of all time.

Confrontations like this are just as impactful as any epic battle in fantasy, and they're settled with social interactions and roleplaying decisions. Your proactive fantasy game will be the same. The conflict that arises as a natural consequence of the tension you've created won't always be violent. In fact, the circumstances of your game will often demand non-violent conflict. The social setting might make violence impossible, for example. In many fantasy TTRPGs, the players expect violent conflict and will often choose it as a quick and direct way to solve conflicts, but you'll find they'll do that less in a proactive game. The variety of the player goals and the overlapping opposing goals make alternative solutions more appealing.

The type and frequency of these non-combat encounters is determined by how your party's goals overlap with the opposing goals of the other factions and NPCs. If your factions have goals about sabotage and theft, the tension between goals will naturally lead to conflict themed around stealth. If your factions have goals about status and interpersonal domination, the tension between goals will naturally lead to conflict about social interaction and court intrigue.

Consider a player character with a goal of "press my claim as the rightful Duke of this land." When the player workshopped that goal with the group, you created one or more overlapping goals and attached them to the factions already present in your world:

the current Duke and his family, the peasants, the local religious institutions, etc. If the current ruling family's goal is to eliminate the threat of your player's claim by proving it is fraudulent, you can expect conflict around locating proper evidence, arguing the claim's legitimacy and digging up dirt. If the current ruling family's goal is to quietly eliminate their PC rival, you can expect conflict expressed as social intrigue and skill challenges to avoid poisonings and unfortunate accidents.

You can layer complexity into your game by considering the goals of other factions with overlapping goals. Imagine the peasants in the above example (a labor and trade organization with no specific leader) want to pay lower tribute rates to the Duke's estate. If the current Duke wants to prove your PC's claim is illegitimate, you might expect some roleplaying interaction with the peasants about whether or not they care about the legitimacy of the Duke. If the current Duke instead wants to quietly eliminate the PC, you can instead explore the social consequences of the Duke's schemes getting out, and how much underhanded murder the peasants will tolerate from a Duke they were already unhappy with.

You can anticipate how these conflicts will play out by examining your player characters' goals and the overlapping goals you created. Consider how the overlap between NPC goals would make certain types of encounters more or less likely. Would another faction or NPC get involved? How many people are interested in the same people, places and objects as the PCs? The way in which these factions pursue goals and collide with the PCs will create the conflict.

If you decide your table doesn't like the number of violent conflicts the party gets into, you can easily increase the number of non-combat encounters and their type by adjusting your faction goals. Here are a few ways you might adjust those goals to better suit the type of game you want to run:

If you just want more non-combat encounters, simply reduce the party's access to violence. Place them in social situations where violence would be punished by authority or disarm them in the presence of certain important people. This is crude but effective and is harder to do with spellcasters.

Shift ownership of the opposing goal to a friendly or neutral faction. Instead of attaching the opposing goal to an insane death-worshiping cult, attach that goal to a friendly faction. They'll need to think about alternative ways to solve the conflict or make a tough decision to choose violence.

Make the death of the opposing side inconsequential. If the opposing goal is about making certain information public, combat is a less appealing option—you can't kill an idea, and all that. Making the information the enemy can change the encounters you'll see.

Increase the power of the opposing side, making direct conflict impossible. Many plucky underdog stories involve social encounters, sabotage, heists and deception because fighting the enemy is impossible—they're too strong. If you can't make the opposing faction stronger, consider attaching the opposing goal to a stronger faction instead.

You may be surprised at how little you need to do to make interesting non-combat encounters. As the players develop their characters and think of next moves, the natural consequences of butting heads with

CASE STUDY

A Rotten Advisor

In one of my 5e games, my players were attempting to win the favor of a powerful king. Unfortunately, he had the classic fantasy royal advisor: a cunning spy, meant to weaken the king and twist him to a greater evil will. This advisor, as the group had discovered, was a shapeshifting dragon that had taken on the guise of an elf, whose goal was to deny any royal aid from the pesky heroes by whispering in the king's ear.

The group understood that a fight could go poorly against the beast, and to attempt to explain the situation to the king might get them thrown out of court. The encounter, then, was a clever discussion in which they attempted to trick the dragon into revealing himself in front of the king. Wordplay, enchanted glasses of wine, attempts to provoke the beast, a few well-placed spells and a lengthy session later, they finally managed to get the beast to slip in his own deception and say something foolish in front of the court.

The aftermath was an encounter in and of itself, but the key to this example is the non-combat driven encounter that resulted from the clashing goals. The players and the dragon had conflicting plans, and as a result of that (and a setting in which violence could end badly for both parties) were forced to resort to more subtle tactics. The encounter was still, ultimately, determined by the players themselves, who were wary of fighting a dragon but knew he had to be defeated by other means. —TF

factions with opposing goals will make for some interesting conflict. A proactive fantasy game is all about setting up the motivations and then seeing where the game takes you, so don't force it.

GOAL-ORIENTED NON-COMBAT ENCOUNTERS

When goals conflict in a non-violent way, we generate encounters that don't transform into battle. These types of conflict can be wildly different from one another, with contrasting paths to victory. In combat, without any additional objective, the primary goals are usually "stay alive" and "kill the enemy." Outside of combat, these

WRITING SOCIAL STATS BLOCKS

Just like I use combat stat blocks to prepare for combat encounters, I'll often use "social stat blocks" to prepare for social encounters. This is a simple collection of relevant information that I organize like a combat stat block so it's easy to read and to find the information I want quickly. I use them for NPCs that I want to roleplay properly, and sometimes for general faction members if I think the party will interact with that faction often.

You should include whatever you think will be useful in your social stat blocks, but I would say the following items are essential:

Goals: Any short-, mid-, and long-term goals should be listed on the social stat block, so you know at a glance how the character will react to any given situation—they'll act to advance those goals.

Faction Affiliation: If your NPC is a member of a faction or is associated with a faction, include that information here. You'll want to know which side they'll choose if factions come into conflict, as well as how what happens to them might affect the larger world.

Tactics: A short description of how this NPC pursues what they want. In a non-combat encounter, are they likely to use deception? Will they make an impassioned plea or a rational argument? These tactics are how the party will learn about the character's goals and personality, so note them here for consistency and ease of use.

Social Skills: If your system uses social checks or social stats, you'll want to list those here as a reference. I like to include what a use of that skill might look like for this character to help me role play better.

You can include anything else you think will be helpful here (appearance, tone, voice, habits, etc). It's all about getting the information you need to run a memorable non-combat encounter in one place. —*JF* types of goals won't gain the needed victory.

A simple way to generate victory conditions is to consider the opposing goals of any parties involved, just like in a combat encounter. As with combat, the friction between different goals is what makes players invested in the encounter. Consider a party trying to secure the public support of a powerful noble. With no goals, the encounter could simply be a few skill checks in which they offer allegiance to the noble. Under the guidance of proactive play, the PCs might have the goal "get a noble's permission to enter the Hall of the Golden Lords" while the noble's goal could be "secure a private parcel my rival needs to be successful in his upcoming business venture." Suddenly, the stakes become very clear, and both groups have a bargaining chip they can use against each other.

Or, instead of a social encounter, perhaps the party is searching for a magical staff, but they need to find it before the thieves guild does. The party's goal may be "use the staff of openings to enter the vault of the ancient dragon" while the thieves guild's goal may be "use the staff of openings to pull off the biggest heist in history." The stakes of the chase have changed, and therefore the approach to finding the staff could as well. The characters could try to throw off the thieves guild with false information on the heist they're hoping to pull off, or the guild could try to tip off the ancient dragon about the PCs' plan.

To prevent your non-combat encounters from dragging on, you'll need to make the victory conditions explicit, with a clear indication of what they entail. Here are a few we use often:

Obtain a promise. In a social negotiation, get the other side to say clearly what they will do. Get promises in writing, or with a witness, just in case.

Extract an apology. Nothing feels better than hearing the words "I'm sorry."

Gain permission to do something from someone. If the players need approval, require them to get it explicitly and in writing, if possible.

Obtain physical evidence of an event. Eyewitness testimony isn't worth much. Find a ledger, birth certificate, smoking gun or similar to prove that something happened.

Negotiate a compromise. Require both parties to clearly and explicitly state what they promise to do for each other. A handshake or a written agreement can seal the deal and signify the task has been completed.

Possess an item. Don't let your players count their proverbial chickens: Make your PCs hold something in their hands before they can say they "own" it.

Win a concession from the other side in an argument. The sweet, sweet sound of someone else saying you're right never gets old. Hearing this means you've won an argument, so make your party work for it.

Win a race. This is one of the clearer ones, but make sure your party knows exactly the bounds of the course and where the finish line is.

If you're having trouble generating unique non-combat encounters based on conflicting goals, use the following table for inspiration.

PC Goal	Enemy Goal	Goal Driven Encounter
Secure the deed for a strategically important piece of land.	Keep the piece of land in neglect and disrepair.	Negotiate for the deed, ward off rivals from the land.
Find a key magic item to bring a companion back from the dead.	Harness the magic of the item to briefly stop the life-death cycle in a small area.	Steal the item without being caught by enemies unable to die.
Retrieve a long-lost ally, now held captive.	Extract crucial information from the ally before they can be found.	Learn the hidden location of the ally by tricking the enemy's servants.
Sway the farmer's guild to avoid using certain magical seeds.	Sow necromantic seeds in the local farms to lay waste to the soil.	Start a public debate between the opposing groups in front of the farmer's guild.
Win the grand prize of a massive footrace.	Rig the competition so that a specific person is guaranteed to win.	Participate in the race while simultaneously avoiding poisoned water, tar-covered ground and time-wasting tricks.
Utilize an old magical archway to create a portal to the soul of an ancient hero.	Use the same archway to siphon souls from Hell directly to monstrous vessels.	Locate the archway and use ancient rituals to twist it into a favorable alignment.

If you take one lesson away from this chapter, let it be this: Conflict in proactive fantasy games can take many forms. Thrilling combat is still one of them but you may find that your group fights less often, too. When the characters are chiefly concerned with achieving their goals, they find creative ways to attain them. This is part of the fun of a proactive game.

Chapter 6

---ᴳ·ᴵ---

REWARDS

W HEN THE DRAGON IS DEAD, the minions are scattered and the princess is saved, there's only one question on the adventurers' minds: How are we gonna divvy up the hoard? Whether in the form of magic items; gold pieces; or sweet, sweet XP; rewards are the fuel that keeps us going in TTRPGs. They aren't the point of playing, necessarily, but they absolutely act as an incentive, and make grinding through life-or-death battles worth the risk. Rewards are what the players need to enact change and pursue more goals.

Players don't pursue goals only for their own sake. The consequences of fulfilling those goals are an important part of TTRPGs, and the most tangible form of that is in rewards.

We think about rewards in two different ways in our proactive games: function and form. The function of a reward is the effect it has on gameplay: it could signal the completion of a goal, introduce a new goal or story element or just be a nice find unrelated to the story. The form of a reward is what type of loot it is: a magic item, useful information, real estate, cold hard cash, etc. Not every reward you create has to tie into your greater network of goals and consequences, but creating rewards that encourage the style of play you want at your table will ensure that's what you get. Players will work hard to complete goals if they know meaningful rewards are waiting for them. In this chapter, we'll cover how to design rewards by choosing a function and form that suits proactive gaming.

The Function of Rewards

Rewards in proactive games are all about the formal completion of goals. Game Masters can use the promise of rewards to move the game in the direction they choose. We'll discuss three functions that rewards serve in proactive games and how to implement each.

GOAL COMPLETION AS ITS OWN REWARD

The simplest reward to introduce is the direct consequence of completing a goal. If a PC wants to obtain a certain sword, learn a powerful spell or claim an ancestral heirloom, then those rewards are the logical conclusion of the goal.

Tie the mechanics of your game to the story by designing goal-related rewards. Make the details of these rewards specific. There are three main benefits to knowing exactly what your goal-related rewards entail ahead of time:

> **You can design better encounters around them.** If you know exactly what the reward is, you'll understand how factions will react or how players might behave when they have it.
>
> **You can incorporate story elements into them.** As you design your rewards, think about the item's past ownership, location and other characteristics. This can either get players involved (by

collaborating on this information) or introduce story hooks or important information for other plot threads.

Manage player expectations. Imagine the disappointment players might feel when they discover that the ring of ultimate power crafted by the dark lord in the heart of a volcano is a simple ring of invisibility. If you know the reward details ahead of time, you can prepare your players and avoid disappointment.

Consult the chart below for ideas on turning story-based goal rewards into mechanical rewards. This chart is made with fantasy settings in mind but could easily be adapted to other settings.

Goal	Related Reward
Steal the magical jewel set into the king's throne.	A fist-sized ruby that allows the wielder to cast *command* once per day without expending a spell slot or materials.
Access the buried archives of a vampire-hunting family.	A +1 whip soaked in holy water that deals explosive damage to undead.
Slay the master swordsman who trained me, then betrayed our clan.	A bonus feat that allows the PC to use the slain swordsman's signature technique.
Secure a trade deal with a foreign miner's guild for high-purity mithril ore.	Raw materials that can be used by a skilled craftsman to enhance armor to grant +1 AC.
Discover the true parentage of the king's heir.	An authentic genealogical chart that proves the actual lineage of the heir.
Win a city's grand gladiatorial tournament.	A gold-plated winner's cup, which can produce enough mead for a hall of heroes to get pleasantly drunk once per week.
Join a secretive and jealous guild of master assassins.	A magical tattoo that prevents the bearer from being targeted by *scry*.
Obtain a blessing from a magical tree in a grove hidden in the wilds.	A magical blessing effect that grants guidance on skill checks related to nature and wilderness survival.

The rewards you present as signals of goal completion can also send characters toward other goals, important places and people or new story elements you want to introduce. In fact, due to the way we've constructed goals, this will usually be the case. By completing one goal, a character will gain the ability to pursue another.

This mechanic works for objects ("obtaining the basilisk fang allows us to pursue our goal of destroying the phylactery"), information ("learning the passphrase to join the Thieves' Guild allows us to infiltrate it, which allows us to pursue our real goal of discovering the identity of its leader") and anything else you can think of. By fleshing out the details of your rewards, you can decide which goals they might be used to pursue and send the party in that direction. We'll examine this idea in more detail in the Rewards as Story Mechanics section on pg. 171.

Rewards as Prizes

A reward isn't always the expected result of completing a goal. After completing a goal, characters often find additional rewards that weren't the primary focus of the goal itself, just a happy accident. Examples of prizes in fiction include Frodo's mithril shirt in *The Lord of the Rings*, Lucy Pevensie's healing potion in *The Chronicles of Narnia* and Luke Skywalker's lightsaber in *Star Wars*.

Prizes are as meaningful as your players wish to make them. They can easily slide into other categories because of their versatile nature: A paladin finds a cursed sword in the dragon's hoard? Who cursed it? What is it linked to? This may or may not be a story the paladin wants to pursue. On the other hand, a massive pile of gold in a vampire's sarcophagus might not end up affecting the story in any major way.

Prizes are often determined by the game system you're using. In a fantasy TTRPG, you may end up with +1 weapons and some potions of healing, while in a horror-based TTRPG, you may wind up with the eyeball of a zombie. This can result in items the players don't use, but it's always possible to pivot and grant the item interesting abilities instead allowing them to be system-generated nothingburgers. A nice unexpected reward can be satisfying enough all on its own.

REWARDS AS STORY MECHANICS

The final function a reward can serve is as a springboard into a new story element. When a reward points players toward new things, it is a story mechanic. When Mat Cauthon finds the ruby-hilted dagger in Shadar Logoth, it sets in motion a new set of long- and mid-term goals for the whole group. Mat's short-term goal of plundering the cursed city was transformed by finding the dagger into a whole host of follow-up goals: "cleanse Mat of the curse," "understand the voices in my head," "recover the missing dagger," etc.

We call the design choice of connecting the reward to a new or different story element a "+1" reward after the numerical bonus used in many TTRPGs. In this case, the reward grants +1 story connections (or +2, or more). This +1 might be an additional object, characteristic or consequence of the reward itself or even just some additional information. Basic examples of reward +1s include:

Introduce a new goal. Connect a new goal to the reward you've introduced. A cursed blade, a piece of jewelry belonging to a powerful noble and a mysterious key all introduce new goals: "cleanse the curse," "return the jewelry" and "find the lock that matches this key." **Make pursuing a current goal possible in a different way.** It's possible for rewards to make certain actions possible that weren't before. If the party wants to assassinate a corrupt noble, obtaining an invitation to a masquerade ball opens a possible avenue for the main goal that was closed before. This is perhaps the easiest way to adjust pacing or to encourage the party to pursue certain encounters.

Resolve or invalidate a goal. Certain rewards might make a goal unworthy of pursuit or resolve it without conflict. If the party owes a gangster money but they are rewarded with an assassin's favor and have the gangster killed, that removes the goal "pay back what we owe." This technique should be used sparingly, when the party is pulled in too many directions at once and feels overwhelmed by the things they want to do.

The business school/political science striver community has a word for a useful concept that we can use here: "actionable." Actionable means that we can use the reward to take some kind of steps toward the connected goal. Your +1 needs to be actionable—it needs to not just imply a connected story element but enable some kind of action that involves that story element. Consider the dragon Smaug. The fire-drake tells us his scales are like "tenfold shields." But we also learn he has a weak spot on his belly. This is the actionable reward (in the form of information) we need to create a plan for bringing down the dragon.

No matter what reward your players earn, the +1 should be like the secret of Smaug's scales. This reward of information about their adversary had the +1 of information that could be used to bring down the dragon and was the key to proceeding with their long-term goal of reclaiming the mountain.

If you're having trouble coming up with +1s for your rewards, consider taking inspiration from the following table. Each one offers a +1 that could tie in to several new goals or story elements.

Goal	Reward	+1
Discover the identity of a masked stalker.	The identity of the person.	Knowledge of a place the person will be at a certain time.
Plunder the treasure of a sealed and warded pyramid.	The treasure of the entombed pharaoh.	A withering curse that affects grave robbers and will bind them to the pharaoh's service in the afterlife.
Pull a magic sword from a stone.	The magic sword.	The right to rule Albion.
Take vengeance on a powerful bandit captain.	Personal satisfaction.	A bounty from the crown for killing the bandit captain and an offer of more work.
Prove the existence of a mythological creature.	The mummified paw of that creature, imbued with certain powers.	A connection via the seller to the hunter who took the trophy.
Destroy evidence of a crime.	The ledger containing the only remaining evidence.	The identity of the rat who made the crime known to the authorities.
Prove devotion to a jealous god.	A divine blessing related to the domain of that god.	A dream in which the god speaks to you and bestows a quest.
Clear the besmirched honor of your disgraced family.	A public apology from the crown for mistreating your family.	The identity of the true perpetrators of the act that brought dishonor to your family.
Win the affection of your true love.	An engagement with that person.	A surprise pregnancy.
Clear a goblin cave near a friendly fantasy village.	The magic scepter of the goblin shaman.	A letter from the goblin's mysterious and clearly villainous benefactor.

Sometimes completing goals will have unintended or even negative consequences. Build these consequences into your rewards as +1s. For example:

Negotiation/Compromise. The party got what they wanted but had to give something up in return. How might this affect the rewards they receive? How might it affect how factions and NPCs treat them afterward?

Pyrrhic Victory. A victory, but at a cost so great it might as well be a loss. Which choices led to this situation? What rewards or +1s might result?

Double Cross. In a goal that involves an NPC or a faction, is it a shared victory? Or might the other forces in play have ulterior motives? How might an opposing faction twist the goal completion or reward to their benefit?

Connecting rewards to story mechanics is an excellent way to control the pace and tone of your narrative. It requires you to think about the reward's place in the world of the game and to have a list of goals, but that'll be easy for you—you've been creating goals since Chapter 1.

Types of Rewards

Once we've thought about the roles a reward can fill, we have to consider what actual rewards can serve those ends. The form of the reward influences the function but is not the exact determining factor. A reward can also serve multiple roles or serve different roles to different characters. In *The Hobbit*, the One Ring falls as a prize to Bilbo Baggins—he unexpectedly finds it, but he doesn't seek it out. It becomes a useful magic item on his adventure. To Frodo, however, the ring serves as a reward only when the goal is completed: "Toss the ring into the cracks of Mount Doom." To Frodo, the true reward of his goal is the completion.

As we look at the primary types of rewards below, we can plan on how they each slot into a different role and how the role itself can change based on the character receiving them.

MAGIC ITEMS

Treasure is the classic fantasy reward. Material items are a method we can use to fulfill our players' goals and make them feel nice about having a big pile of stuff in the process.

We need to give our players magic items that assist them in their goals, pushing them further into proactive play. Some items may be overpowered, some may be useless, some may be useful but cannot be wielded by your players and some may only have situational utility.

First and foremost, know your party's goals, then understand how useful an item would be in fulfilling them. In a group of mages, a flaming sword isn't going to excite anyone. When you reward the party, you want the item to be relevant enough to warrant use. With more situational items, you can ensure they'll be useful at some point. A potion that protects from cold? Perhaps they have a goal that requires fighting ice elementals.

An RPG that uses items as a form of character progression will invariably have some massive list of items for GMs to choose from, but when rewarding our players to encourage further agency, it often feels like you're required to invent new items wholesale for your players.

It is always easier to alter than to create. If there is an item close to what you need, it's easier to tweak that than to make an entirely new one. For example, if your wizard has a powerful affinity for ice, you can reflavor a fire-based magic item so it deal cold damage instead. In addition, improving a powerful item can be a goal in itself.

A goal-anchoring item (often called an artifact) should, in fact, evolve over time—if the character gets an item or artifact at the close of a campaign or by level 20, there's very little payoff for the wait. They use a brand new weapon for a session or two and then it's over. But to find a weapon early on, deepen your connection to it, tinker with it, grow with it and ultimately see it multiply in power as a trusted companion—this is what makes a character earn their weapon. Grabbing it from a dragon at the last second feels anticlimactic.

Such an artifact could start as a simple weapon related to the characters' abilities—a sword with a +1 to hit. Over time, it may gain more abilities as the character levels up. These changes should occur during major successes and moments of growth, which often overlap with the character's goals or are related to them in some way. As the character grows, so too does their bond with their artifact.

INFORMATION

Information rewards are usually highly character-specific, less often party-specific and rarely faction-specific. In other words, the value of a piece of information varies wildly based on who knows it.

Therefore, information rewards should be used to signify the completion of a goal. The important thing to realize here is that simply knowing something usually doesn't signify the end of a character arc. On the contrary, information is nearly always an intermediate step for characters looking to pursue a greater goal. As a result, information rewards should always be designed with a +1 that allows a PC to act on the information they've just gained.

If you're having trouble thinking of some +1s to attach to your information rewards, try rolling on this table.

Player Goal	+1 Information Idea
Discover the identity of a mysterious or important person.	The last known location of that person.
Discover the location of a long-lost item or person.	A map that shows the way to the location.
Learn a powerful spell or technique.	The identity of a known master of that technique or spell.
Discover the identity of a person who committed some wrong against the PC.	The identity of another victim of that wrongdoer.
Find the true meaning of an important prophecy.	A corroborating prophecy from a different culture or religion.
Prove that a well-established fact is false.	The identity of a person who is intentionally spreading the falsehood.
Divine the will or intention of a god.	The opposing intention of another god.
Locate a chosen one.	The location of an old religious order dedicated to training the chosen one.
Obtain a trade secret or profitable market information.	The identity of another person who knows the same information.
Obtain blackmail information on an important figure.	A location and time where proof for that information can be obtained.

Other Rewards

While treasure is what most players think of when they think of rewards, utility rewards make up a great portion of the loot in a fully proactive fantasy game. A utility reward is any reward that's useful because it allows a player to take an action they couldn't before or makes that action easier. A magic sword is a treasure reward, but a map that tells you where to find the sword is a utility reward, for example.

Goal	Utility Item
Destroy a powerful magical artifact.	The forge in which it was made.
Return to their homeland.	A ship or wagon.
Enter a powerful magic vault.	The Key of Ten Thousand Ages.
Defend or mentor an important young person.	A secluded home with a few traps to deter intruders.
Claim an ancestral birthright or fortune.	The ceremonial crown of the kingdom.
Destroy or neutralize a powerful person.	A rare fruit they're extremely allergic to.
Conquer a city.	A collection of trebuchets.
Marry the king.	Deeds to a collection of lands for use as a dowry.

A utility item is only as useful for as long as you need it. This is not always a bad thing—if the player has proven the corrupt king was evil, and the proof of his crimes isn't useful anymore, it won't have much of a negative impact on the players. But when the keep their ally died for falls into ruin because they never have a chance to use it, it can be disappointing. As Game Masters, we have the power to change that. The keep is attacked! Refugees need a place to stay! You need a place to imprison your enemies! There are any number of new scenarios you can introduce that keep your utility rewards useful and beneficial to your players, particularly the ones they fought tooth and nail to obtain in the first place.

Remember, this doesn't apply to every reward. Constantly forcing a character to reuse their old rewards isn't exciting, but a middle ground that keeps useful things useful and lets the junk fade into the background is what keeps the game interesting.

Chapter 7

ENCOUNTERS

THROUGHOUT THIS BOOK, we've focused on practical actions you can take put players at the center of every session: How to set goals, how to add conflict and how to design locations, combat and rewards around character goals. Now it's time to put it all together by finalizing your encounters.

An "encounter" is a conflict that happens between your players and the forces that oppose them. It usually involves rolling dice: combat and social interactions are the most frequent encounters you'll see. Encounters are the main way your players will interact with the world of your game, and a session is made up of a few encounters strung together with some snacks and puns in between. They're the culmination of everything you've been working on as you've read this book: expressions of the intersection of your party's goals (Chapter 1) and the goals of those who oppose them (Chapters 2 and 3) in a place (Chapter 4) where that conflict (Chapter 5) can be settled by someone winning it (Chapter 6).

This chapter will guide you through the process of collecting the who, where, what, how and why that you'll need to maximize the impact of every encounter.

ENCOUNTER DESIGN

Encounters emerge from the overlap between your players' goals and the goals of the villains and factions that oppose or are competing with them. If you've followed our advice thus far, then you should have a general sense of what your encounters might look like. Whether you're creating a combat encounter, a skill challenge or a social situation, you'll need to collect a few pieces of information in one place to have everything you need to run the encounter. When in doubt, use the following steps to cut through the noise:

1. Review your players' goals.

Before you design encounters, you'll need to know what goals your players are currently working on. You should have a current list of these at all times (read more about this list and see the checklist for character goals in Chapter 1 [pg. 22]). Over the course of a campaign there will be multiple encounters that players will face in order to accomplish each of their goals. For now, pick the one your players are interested in actively pursuing.

2. Determine which factions have goals that overlap with your players' goals.

Look through the factions you've designed for your world. Which faction has interests that overlap with the player goal you picked in Step 1? Read more about faction goals, see examples and work through the faction checklist in Chapter 2 (pg. 48).

3. Pick a few NPC goals that oppose your players' goals.

Look through the NPCs that are affiliated with the factions you picked in the last step. Which of these NPCs have goals that conflict with the player goal you're designing an encounter around? Are there allies that might work with the PCs to accomplish this goal?

How might a patron the PCs know get involved? Pick one or more goals belonging to your NPCs that conflict with the player goal you've chosen. Read more about NPC goals and work through the ally, villain and patron checklist in Chapter 3 (pg. 74).

4. Choose where this encounter will take place.

Consider where the party could go to pursue their goals that will bring them into conflict with the factions and NPCs opposing them. Think of the locations you've attached to your players' goals and choose the location you've designed around this goal. Read about backward location design and how to craft your locations to make them suitable for these conflicts in Chapter 4 (pg. 106).

5. Determine what type of conflict is likely to occur and how the other side will fight.

Based on the opposing goals you've chosen, what type of conflict will occur? Is it the type of disagreement that can only be solved with violence? If not, might violence happen anyway? Determine the mechanical details of each enemy, balance combat encounters appropriately and create social stat blocks if necessary. Consider the tactics the enemies might use to get what they want and how hard they are willing to fight for it.

ENCOUNTER DESIGN CHECKLIST

Here's a quick checklist for encounter design. If you need to brush up on one of the topics, check the chapters listed.
- Who's in conflict with your players? (Ch 1, 2 and 3)
- Where can that conflict be resolved? (Ch 4)
- What form might that conflict take? (Ch 5)
- Why are the opposing sides fighting? (Ch 6)

Once you know these things, your encounter is ready to run.

Review Your Players' Goals

You should have a running list of these at all times.

Goal Guidelines:

1. Each character should have multiple goals.
2. Goals should be varied in length.

3. Goals must be achievable.
4. Goals must have consequences for failure.
5. Goals must be fun to pursue.

Which Factions Have Goals That Overlap With PC Goals?

Faction goals are created by first deciding a faction's:

1. Identity
2. Area of operation
3. Power level
4. Ideology

Then **select faction goals** that concern the same people, places and objects as PC goals.

Which NPCs From the Faction Oppose the PCs Directly?

NPC goals are created in direct response to PC goals (allies and villains) or are more personality-driven interpretations of faction goals (patrons).

Select the NPCs from the involved factions that have goals that concern the same people, places and objects as PC goals.

Decide Where This Conflict Will Take Place

Custom-design a location for your goal by considering:

1. Is this goal tied to a location already?
2. If not, where might this goal succeed or fail?
3. Why was this place created?
4. Who is present?

What type of conflict will likely occur?

For a combat encounter...

1. Decide on the mechanical details of the enemies.
2. Decide the stakes of the fight and what the enemies are trying to accomplish.
3. Determine their tactics from their goals.

For a non-combat encounter...

1. Decide who is present at the encounter.
2. Decide what strategies they will use.
3. Determine what success looks like for all involved parties.

6. Determine the rewards for completing the encounter.

Using your players' goals as a guide, determine what a satisfying reward for prevailing in this encounter would be. Consider the consequences of this goal being resolved and decide how to telegraph them, if necessary. Read about designing rewards and considering consequences in Chapter 6 (pg. 166).

7. Prepare your materials and necessary player aides.

Decide on the materials you'll need (such as miniatures, props or battle maps) to run the encounter. If you use battle maps, use one that matches the location of your encounter or create a new one. If you don't use battle maps, think about how you'll communicate the appearance and atmosphere of the encounter to your players. If the conflict is complicated or calls for drama, consider preparing handouts or props to make the game flow better and build excitement.

Remember that the encounter, not the adventure, is the fundamental unit of play. String enough encounters together and an adventure with a very clear arc will emerge from the conflict and actions players take to resolve it. Once you've done a few of these, it becomes very easy to do them on the spot, so don't be afraid to follow the game wherever the players want to take it. That's the point of the proactive RPG system!

ANOTHER KIND OF ENCOUNTER: YOU AND YOUR PLAYERS

None of your planning and preparation matters much if the game goes off the rails right away. One of the downsides to putting player agency at the core of your game is that players are often unpredictable. Every Game Master has worked for hours on some exciting dungeon only to have the players walk right past it on their way to waylay a pilgrim with a shiny belt buckle, or some other unforeseeable distraction. Luckily, refocusing your game on player agency and character choices also helps alleviate the problems that player agency can create. Since we have a clear idea of what the characters are after, we can prepare material around those desires—as long as they stay true to them.

What follows is a bit of advice alongside some suggestions we've found effective for running these types of games. No matter how much planning you do, the best-designed game can be boring if it's run poorly, so it's important to bring everything together at the table by encouraging proactive play and discouraging reactive play.

HAVE PLAYERS DESIGN ADVENTURES FOR YOU

It's easy to get stuck in a mindset of "the player's job is to play through the content the Game Master prepares." We hope we've convinced you to leave that mindset behind.

One of the easiest ways to do that is to enlist your players' help in designing content. This doesn't need to be a formal request ("OK Timmy, please create a dungeon for next time"). Instead, enlist your players by first asking them to explain their goals to you. Take some time before or after the session (I usually do this to start the session, after we've all sat down and caught up) to go through a character's goals. What are their short-, mid- and long-term goals? How close are they to those goals? Are they encouraged or discouraged? What would it look like when they reach those goals?

The last question is the most important one. It tells us what the player thinks of as the goal's "completion," and that's what we should try to design our encounters around. Ask follow-up questions about what obstacles the player expects, how hard they think they'll have to fight and more to see what kind of encounters the player is expecting. You can then choose to implement those, build on them or reject them in favor of something else just to keep them on their toes.

For example, consider a player whose goal is to find a certain sword that is sacred to her holy order. Her character doesn't know where the sword is, only that it was stolen by a rival faction of cultists. She explains that her character is frustrated by how long it's taking to find the sword and has the short-term goal of interrogating a cultist. In this situation, you might ask what she wants to get out of the cultist: an exact location? The name of someone who might know where the sword is? You might also ask where she is going to find this cultist. Based on her answer, you can start to design encounters around her expectations. If she says she wants to beat it out of a cultist, you'll need to design a few combat encounters with the cult, as well as have a sense of how members of the holy order might feel about one of their congregants using torture to achieve a personal goal. If the player instead says she wants to infiltrate the cult and convince one of them to spill the beans, you'll need to design some social and stealth encounters. In this way, the player is helping you design the game simply by expressing her ideas for pursuing her goal.

As you play, you'll get a feel for what your players like and the encounters they expect. Jot down a note whenever a player says something like, "What if X happens because we did Y?" You can turn these into encounters later if it fits what is going on behind the scenes. If it's a good idea and you can retcon your existing plans easily, just make that change on the fly. Your players are a constant source of imagination and investment. Use them as often as you feel comfortable by having them explain and elaborate on their goals, then design your encounters around their ideas and expectations.

To see these principles in action, run the adventure on pg. 196. It's designed to demonstrate how this works in practice, and you'll be able to complete a series of workbook-like activities (we promise it's fun) to experience what it's like to ask your players to help design encounters.

ASK INTERESTING CHARACTER QUESTIONS

In most combat-heavy games, we tend to think of our characters as stat blocks. This is logical—we are not in a play or book. But we lose something by not developing our characters or imagining them as sentient beings with wants, needs, bonds and flaws in the way a playwright or novelist might, especially in a proactive fantasy game. In proactive fantasy, we rely on our players to generate interesting goals for their characters to pursue. How can they do that if they don't know their characters deeply? Well enough to generate good goals for them and challenge them to think about their characters in new ways? The easiest way to make sure they do is by opening your sessions with character questions: simple questions that players may not have considered. This simple way of kicking off your session gives players a chance to ease into roleplay while thinking critically about the way their character views the world, and helps cement each character in the minds of other players. Game Masters who emphasize roleplaying will tell you they often see a pattern over the course of their campaigns: characters going from being loot-hungry maniacs who are also good fighters to varied, complex and interesting people. In our games, we attribute this to the character questions we throw at them and the ways they decide to work their answers into the game. If your players are having trouble generating meaningful character goals or if you just want them to get to know their characters better, use the questions in the table opposite. You can have them answer the questions in character (as in, in the fiction of the game the characters are talking to each other and this topic comes up) or out of character (as in, the other characters don't know this about the speaking player's character but might discover it over time).

1d20 Character Development Questions

1d20	
1	Which character in the party do you trust the most? The least?
2	What will you do when you retire? When do you think that will be?
3	Who is your role model? Who do you try to imitate in your adventures?
4	What is your greatest strength? Your greatest failing?
5	What would you like to change about yourself?
6	What is the greatest adventure you've ever been on?
7	What is your proudest accomplishment as an adventurer? Overall?
8	What is your sense of humor like? What makes you laugh?
9	If you weren't an adventurer, what would you do instead?
10	Have you ever done hard time? What were you locked up for? If not, what do you think about people who were?
11	Are you good at cooking? What do you cook?
12	If you could go back in time and change something, what would it be?
13	What is the longest you have ever gone without sleep? Why did you do it?
14	What is your morning routine while out on an adventure? How about in town?
15	Have you ever been in love?
16	Who knows you best in the world?
17	Where does your name come from? Why are you named that?
18	Do you have any irrational fears? What are they?
19	How superstitious are you? Do you have any unusual spiritual beliefs?
20	What does your perfect day look like and why?

If these sound like they were ripped from an internet quiz or a mommy blog, it's because they were. We get all our best questions from these sources, and they are a bottomless well of ideas to draw on for your campaigns. You don't necessarily need determine whether a PC is a

Monica, Rachel or Phoebe, but asking players to answer these questions for their characters is a great way to get them out of their comfort zone so they develop their character. Remember, the goal here is to develop a character with strong ideals and who wants something badly enough that they will fight for it. If a player always answers with "I don't know" or has a weak or non-committal answer, they may need some extra encouragement. Don't forget to always follow up with "Why?"

IMPROVISE

Improvisation is an unbelievably useful skill (and often a necessity) when running a game. Players going off the beaten path and subverting hours of preparation is a classic fish story among Game Masters for a reason—often recounted as legend born from terrifying, white-knuckled reality. In every encounter you will be forced to improvise an answer to a question in some way, shape or form. There is no way to improve at this other than to practice, but there are a number of well-worn techniques improvisational actors employ, which we can apply to our games. These techniques have the added benefit of letting you adjust to new situations, letting your players choose their path and enforcing their role as partial leaders of the story.

Start with a classic: "Yes, and" is the root of all good improv. The concept, is simple: When you respond to a question or attempt at action with a simple "no," it immediately shatters the momentum and excitement. Instead, responding with "yes, and" (or possibly "yes, but") not only keeps the story moving but continues to give the players their say in the direction of the session. It keeps the story and challenges moving forward. Nothing murders the momentum of a game more than a flat-out "no." We want to improve player proactivity as much as possible, and to achieve this end, we need to encourage their ideas, not shut them down. This typically requires coming up with what "yes, and" would mean on the fly.

As a Game Master, "yes, and" can apply to the mechanics of the games we play. When a player asks if they can shoot through one goblin and hit another, the standard rules of 5e would say no. There's nothing wrong with finding a compromise, a skill check or house rule that allows the player to continue on. Experienced players will help you navigate the ground between what's good for the story and what's written in the rulebook, but at the end of the day the decision always rests with you. When you can, rule in favor of your players.

The rule of "yes, and" however, primarily applies to non-mechanical abilities and interactions. When a player wants to persuade a noble to grant them a favor, that noble's "no" grinds their plans to a halt. Accepting a player's actions allows the story to move forward instead of stalling out. When their attempts are far-fetched or less successful, your answer may change to "yes, but." This serves a similar function—it keeps the momentum of an encounter moving forward, toward a resolution, but it adds a new twist, challenge or complication. "Yes, but the noble's rival is offended you didn't approach them instead." "Yes, but the noble asks for something in return." "Yes, but one of your rivals overhears."

While the 5e system is fairly binary (something succeeds or fails, and only the dice can decide), numerous TTRPG systems include a sort of gray area—partial failure or partial success. It's "yes, and" or "yes, but" with an associated dice mechanic. If you're in a binary yes/no, hit/miss, pass/fail system, consider adding a spread to your DCs. If wooing the nobleman to your cause is DC 18, consider that anything over a 15 would get him on board, but if it's less than the DC, there are powerful strings attached. Additionally, if players exceed a DC by a fair amount, add some "and" by offering more than they asked for.

Fail Forward

The most important path improv can provide is one forward from failure. When a character fails a check or falls short of accomplishing a goal (as they should sometimes, that's the way games go), they should not lose their intent entirely. As with the partial success rules, a failure should only present new challenges, not close every avenue. If a character fails a check to climb a rope, they shouldn't plummet off the cliff and instantly die from 20d6 damage—that's boring, unfair and reduces the character's life to a single die roll. The rope could fray, the wind could blow them to a new location, they could catch themselves on the cliff and have to climb rope-free up the rest—all of these options are essential for the momentum of a story. Most importantly, failure can often be an important aspect of a goal. As discussed in Chapter 1, a character failing at a goal can be just as important as a character succeeding, as it causes new and interesting story beats.

At a certain point, one needs to wonder when to stop. Boblin the Goblin has rolled 5 natural 1s in a row: How is he not dead? That line can only be found by instinct. But even when a player objectively fails their goal, that failure can still open new challenges. Boblin failed to cross the river? He's been dragged by its current deep underground, emptying out into the well of a dungeon far below the surface. The wizard fails to conduct a powerful ritual? Powerful motes of sentient magic spew forth and flee, and they must be collected to empower more magic.

Failure should never be the end of a challenge, just the start of a new one. As discussed, a common shorthand for this technique is "no, but," a way to describe failure and push the narrative in a new direction. "No, you don't persuade the noble, but his rival approaches after seeing him reject you." "No, you don't make it to shore, but the storm has swept you to a strange new country."

If your player fails at their first big swing at a major goal, don't let them give up on the goal itself. Apply the necessary fallout from failure (a bruised tailbone, a broken sword, a shattered ego) then present options that allow them to pursue the goal in a different way (through the much more dangerous Mines of Sorrow, partnered with a band of undesirables, in a way that would force them to break several very old but still very enforceable laws).

CHEAT LIKE A GAME MASTER

The most important part of being a Game Master is knowing how to cheat (cheat nobly, at any rate). We won't get into the ethics of fudging dice, but the basis of most TTRPGs is to make the world feel real. When we use improv, there's the possibility we compromise the feeling of a grounded world where actions have consistent consequences with one that feels a little too impromptu or spontaneous. For some games, this is perfectly fine. The inverse can be true as well—a world that's too rigid or that doesn't change regardless of the actions taken by your players is one that feels cold and lifeless. That's why it's our practice to do a bit of planning (namely the sort outlined in previous chapters), a fair amount of plotting (primarily considering how player goals will interact with each other once obstacles are introduced) and then kick things to our players knowing that the only thing they can break is the will of the NPCs we control.

Lists are your best friend. NPC names, locations and even accents can help quickly throw together a character on the fly. "Town guard's name? Let me check my notes." Cross them off the list. In the same vein: random online generators and roll tables are also great to deploy when a question you don't immediately know the answer to comes up. There is no shame whatsoever in lifting names from a generator, as long as it's for your home game—there are thousands of them, and keeping one on a tab of your laptop during a game saves both stress and time.

TAKE A DETAILED PRE-/POST-GAME ACCOUNTING

We've detailed a hefty amount of information to help you run a proactive game, but if we're being honest, it's a lot to keep track of. Accounting is crucial to most games—without a tiny bit of work before and after, how does anything happen in between? Taking quick notes to remember events, the actions of various factions and steps for future sessions are all elements that keep you sane in-game. Below is a list of steps you can try before and after sessions (another useful checklist to refer to can be found in Chapter 1). Use it. Your future self will thank you.

BEFORE

1. Review relevant goals. Observe player goals, check what your players were interested in next and plan encounters accordingly.

2. Prepare the battle maps, if applicable. I have had GMs that would only draw maps on the fly. That only works if done quickly and smoothly, which means it rarely works. If a battlefield must be drawn, have it done before the session.

3. Review relevant information. The last thing you want is to be stumbling over important events that only happened a session ago—keep your important information in mind (it will probably mostly be useful in jogging your players' memory, in all honesty).

4. Prepare cheat sheets and websites. Names, places, people, accents, shops—have them ready, or risk a clunky transition while you dig out a character sheet or wait for a site to load.

5. Outsource the recap. Assign a new player each week to write up a recap of the previous session to distribute before the next one begins. This helps you track the things that stuck with your player(s), while also taking this aspect of session prep off your plate. You could also have a different player summarize the events that led them to where they are as part of the session intro to further solidify where you are and where they want to go.

AFTER

1. Write a brief outline of the session. Just something short, unless you feel like writing a novel. Primary people the party met, places they went, people they killed (this is my favorite when there are necromancer villains—keep handy!). If you've asked another player to keep track of that week's recap, they can take this job off your plate—but you can also create your own, comparing your own memory of important events to theirs to gain even more intel.

2. Check your clocks. Or whatever tool you use for factions—double check everything is accounted for. This is also when you determine the ramifications of any clock-based goal completed off-screen.

3. Check with your players. This is the most important one! If you heed a single piece of advice in this section, it should be this: Ask your players what they want to do next.

Now that you have all the tools we can provide for running your proactive fantasy games, it's time to put what you've learned into practice. What follows is a one-shot adventure designed to introduce you to this style of play by walking through each step of the process and specifically calling out when something might be different than you're used to. Don't just read this adventure, actually play it!

PLUNDERING IN PINE HOLLOW

─◦─ᵴ·ᴣ─◦─

A PROACTIVE ONE-SHOT ADVENTURE

NOW THAT YOU'VE GOT A CLEAR IDEA of how reframing your game to be about player goals can transform your experience, it's time to see these principles in action. It can be difficult to design an adventure for your table with all of this new proactive roleplay knowledge in mind, especially since your players' goals should determine the course of your game. So we've compromised, experimented and tinkered to present an adventure using our approach for you to adapt to your table.

The result of all this experimentation takes the form of something like a workbook. We'll start by establishing a somewhat generic fantasy setting in which several factions vie for power. Then, you'll sit down with your players and help them pick goals according to the guidelines provided on pg. 39. These goals are necessarily open-ended since they'll tie directly into the setting we lay out in this chapter, but they will constitute a good example of how to tie player goals to your settings.

From there, you'll develop NPCs by connecting them to the player goals you've selected. This will ensure the NPCs are directly involved in the same scenarios as your players: a delicious recipe for conflict and dramatic tension. It's best to complete this step together with your players so you can all see how the world unfolds in response to specific goals the players chose. This will also help communicate what is different about proactive play and help get the players invested.

Then you'll create settings, again using your players' goals to populate each location and determine its significance. Your players should also be present for this step, though you may wish to conceal some details to preserve the element of surprise.

The next step is reviewing the combat information you're likely to need and deciding on the tactics each enemy will use, based on what you've outlined for each NPC and the forces they command (Note: We reference a few stat blocks from the 5e SRD). Review the rewards at stake for each goal and decide what those look like for your game.

Finally, you'll consider your party's goals—what they're most excited about achieving—and poll them about what to do first. This will help you set up your first few encounters, which you'll do by organizing information you already have. From there, you can start the game using the suggestion for the introduction on pg. 229 and then just let the players loose.

As you read and work through this process, notice how nearly everything is determined by the players. While we've provided the setting to make something like this possible, you'll make the necessary changes in reaction to the players' choices, instead of prompting them to react to your choices.

The Setting

The small town of Pine Hollow is located in the foothills of an old mountain range, tucked away in the shade of a sharp ridge. Old pine trees cover the slopes, and needles blanket the forest floor up to the edge of town. Across the hollow (or holler, depending on whom you ask) are the ancient ruins of a fort, blackened by dragonfire and overtaken by the forest. A swift-flowing river has cut a shallow canyon into the limestone and winds down the mountain, allowing workers to easily send ore and precious stones downriver on barges to more profitable markets. Though the mines were once a great source of wealth for the area, a combination of the veins running dry and following a dragon attack last autumn means the mining companies have mostly left.

Pine Hollow is sparsely populated, with only a few hundred full-time residents. Seasonal laborers of all races and creeds come to work the meager mines and barges in the warmer months. Adventurers are drawn to the region too, knowing the dwarves who used to call these hills home left caches of valuables in the mines when the galena veins dried up and the miners moved on. Some mining guilds hold out hope that there are still valuable minerals buried deeper in the mountain. Others disagree.

CREATING FACTIONS

The two main factions with whom the parties will interact most in this adventure are the Chosen of Ivrut (the Chosen) and the Brasscrown Mountain Trading Company (BMTC). When the adventure starts, the two factions are on the brink of armed violence against each other due to their opposing goals.

We'll create these factions (and a few more: the Pine Hollow Town Council and Those Left Behind) now, with less input from the group than the rest of the setting will take. These factions will pursue their goals with or without involvement from the players (represented by the clocks on the Cheat Sheet on pg. 232). After the players have chosen their goals, we'll create complementaary faction goals. Later, we'll create NPCs, locations, combat encounters and rewards that are directly influenced by the party's goals.

THE BRASSCROWN MOUNTAIN TRADING COMPANY

The Brasscrown Mountain Trading Company consists of ore prospectors, miners, opportunists and treasure hunters working (well, hoping) to extract precious metals out of the earth. The faction has the following characteristics:

1. Faction Identity: The BMTC is a labor and trade faction. Members range from honest prospectors to greedy opportunists, depending on the goals of the players. They spend their time surveying the mountainside and extracting precious materials.

2. Area of Operation: The BMTC is an extension of a much larger mining guild, but because of Pine Hollow's isolated location, they have little contact with their parent guild and are mostly limited to Pine Hollow and its surroundings.

3. Power Level: The BMTC is filled with dozens of down-on-their-luck hopefuls trying to catch a break, but not all are loyal to the company. The gold and influence the company wields, and its connections (though limited) to its larger guild, make it a formidable faction. It is roughly equal in power to the Chosen.

4. Ideology: The BMTC venerates wealth and daring, valuing bold members who take big risks to access ore deposits. Many of the mines are unstable, and those willing to risk a cave-in can potentially gain a great reward—even if they lose a few limbs along the way.

The BMTC is linked to a larger faction, and their goal is to export ore for a profit. They aim to revitalize the mining operations in Pine Hollow (long-term) by exposing vast swaths of precious ore with their geomancers, stripping away upper layers of earth. We'll start a clock for that goal so we know if/when they start blasting. They oppose the Chosen because the cult is preventing prospectors from accessing areas that likely hold precious metals.

THE CHOSEN OF IVRUT

The Chosen of Ivrut are a religious faction that worship Ivrut, the mighty dragon who, 50 years ago, charred Pine Hollow Keep to a crisp. The faction has the following characteristics:

1. Faction Identity: The Chosen of Ivrut are religious and/or criminal. They operate outside the scope of the law, relying on zealous followers and subterfuge to grasp at wealth and power. Depending on player goals, the Chosen could be presented as an enterprising but fairly neutral thieves' guild or a dangerous cult hell-bent on sundering anyone who stands in their way.

2. Area of Operation: The Chosen are fairly limited in scope, operating only near the charred remains of Pine Hollow Keep. Those who have seen the aftermath of dragon fire are sometimes led by the experience to cower and prostrate themselves before its immense power, and the Chosen set up camp at this region's ground zero.

3. Power Level: While numbering only a few dozen, the Chosen are sneaky and subversive. They can also gain great power through pacts and magic items. Wealth is a great asset to them, providing not only the power to manipulate the political landscape but also the means to wield the mysteries of divine magic through dragon worship. They are approximately equal in power to the Brasscrown Mountain Trading Company, but on their own, they likely aren't strong enough to seize control of Pine Hollow.

4. Ideology: The Chosen venerate wealth and power above all else, in keeping with the dragon they revere. Brutal ambition is venerated as a virtue in the cult's holy scribblings, which means betrayals are commonplace. The Chosen also believe the hoard of Ivrut is guarded by a powerful curse, and only their leader can dispel it in order to access the treasure safely.

The Chosen of Ivrut are a local faction, so their goals concern Pine Hollow and the surrounding mountains. Their aim is to find the lost hoard of Ivrut, buried deep in the mountain (long-term). We'll start a clock for this goal so we know if/when the hoard has been accessed. They oppose the BMTC because blowing off the top of the mountain (a BMTC goal) in search of minerals would certainly damage Ivrut's hoard or, at the least, make accessing it more difficult. As your party develops and your game goes on, consider other long-term goals for the Chosen that concern the same people, places and objects as the party's goals.

PINE HOLLOW TOWN COUNCIL

The Pine Hollow Town Council is a small group of rulers elected by general vote each year. Since the settlement is small, rule generally falls to the same few people time and time again, though with their limited power, they have precious little influence compared to the other factions. The faction has the following characteristics:

1. Faction Identity: The Council is a government faction. They set the laws in the area and enforce them using their small militia.

2. Area of Operation: The Council's power is centered in the town of Pine Hollow itself. While their power technically extends across the entire mountain, they only have enough soldiers to keep order in the town.

3. Power Level: Although they decree the laws in Pine Hollow, they rarely have the power to enforce them. The Council is weaker than the Chosen and the BMTC but is slightly stronger than Those Left Behind due to their organizational strengths.

4. Ideology: The Council believes strongly in tradition and order. They obey the structures of past systems, and when things are in disarray, attempt to quell the cause of chaos by deploying a modest troop of mediocre guards.

As a force of stability, the Council wants to remove the Chosen from the old keep and stop the BMTC from blowing the top off the mountain. Not all members are aligned on this, and you can assume there are Council members secretly aligned with the Chosen or the BMTC. Maybe even both.

THOSE LEFT BEHIND

Those Left Behind are a faction only in the loosest sense of the term. They murder and cannibalize, and their united hatred for the surface-dwellers makes them a force in their own right, as do the strange magical mutations that manifest within them. These mountain-dwellers were originally workers, accidentally sealed away in the mines during Ivrut's attack. They have now gone irreversibly mad in the darkness. After decades, a few have found small tunnels leading back to the surface world they now abhor.

1. Faction Identity: Those Left Behind is a criminal faction. They rely on thievery and murder to get luxuries for life below ground.

2. Area of Operation: Those Left Behind are extremely active underground venturing to the surface rarely and only at night. After years of darkness, the sun hurts their eyes. They also abhor the inhabitants of Pine Hollow, and seeing them in the flesh sends Those Left Behind into a rage.

3. Power Level: Due to their lack of organization, Those Left Behind are effectively the weakest faction in Pine Hollow, but they possess abilities that should not be underestimated.

4. Ideology: Those Left Behind value vengeance above all else, and what better way to extract that vengeance than by claiming the most prized possession of their enemies: the power to which they cling. Their time underground has made them bitter, insane and permanently changed in a visceral way.

A monstrous faction, Those Left Behind hate the sun, have no leader and exist in this adventure to add a wildcard faction to encounters inside the mountain. Their immediate goal is to drive all trespassers out of their tunnels and back up into the light. If you want a more complicated and aggressive game, consider having Those Left Behind declare war on the surface.

CHARACTER GOAL GENERATION

Your players should bring characters of 3rd level to the table before choosing goals, though some players may instead want to pick goals before creating a character. To choose goals, each player should roll 2d4 and consult goals from the tables that follow: Each player should have one goal from the table on the opposite page, and one from the table on pg. 206. Alternatively, have your players pick goals from the tables instead of rolling.

There should be some overlap in your group of goals. This will bind the characters together and give them common cause. It's unlikely, though possible, that some characters won't have goal overlap with the rest of the group, so don't be afraid to tweak goals if necessary to create better party cohesion.

The following goals are location-related. After selecting a goal, the player should choose a location from the choices in brackets. The players should then discuss the details of their goals with the group, including you. Why does their character want to accomplish this? What are the details of the spell, the setting or the item? Players may decide to choose the same locations here to increase party cohesion.

1d4	Code	Goal
1	Goal A	Defend [The Ruins of Pine Hollow Keep/The Collapsed Mineshaft] from an impending attack.
2	Goal B	Learn a powerful spell that has been sealed away in [The Lost Hoard of Ivrut/The Ruins of Pine Hollow Keep].
3	Goal C	Seize control of [The Ruins of Pine Hollow Keep/the local tavern].
4	Goal D	Obtain a certain powerful magic item stored at [The Ruins of Pine Hollow Keep/The Lost Hoard of Ivrut].

The following goals are related to the two main factions, the Chosen of Ivrut and the Brasscrown Mountain Trading Company. After selecting a goal, the player should choose which of these two factions that goal concerns. The players should then discuss the details of these goals with the group: Why are the characters interested in these factions? What do they hope to achieve by accomplishing these things? How are they related to the character's larger story?

1d4	Code	Goal
1	Goal E	Discover the identity of the leader of [The Chosen/The BMTC].
2	Goal F	Bring home a missing family member who has joined [The Chosen/The BMTC].
3	Goal G	Slay a lieutenant of [The Chosen/The BMTC].
4	Goal H	Become a member of [The Chosen/The BMTC].

As your players fill in the details of these rough goals, don't be afraid to make changes. As long as your players are pursuing roughly similar goals together, the game will be fun. Make the changes required to suit your table.

CREATING NPCS

Now that your players have decided which goals their characters will pursue, we'll spend some time on additional details to ensure dramatic conflict and interesting encounters, starting with designing NPCs.

NOTE: *The character profiles below are missing some information that you'll need to decide with your group. Each blank has a number associated with it. For each blank, check the corresponding numbered steps that follow to determine this information. Fill in the details as you make decisions. When every blank is full, you're ready to generate goals for the character.*

VICROS DRAKEBLOOD

Vicros Drakeblood is a half-elf preacher and religious figure who leads the Chosen of Ivrut and is a (1) _____. As the leader of the Chosen, Vicros wields absolute authority over several dozen cultists, including (2) _____.
Vicros hasn't gotten his hands on the dragon's hoard yet, but he does receive weekly tithes from his loyal followers, including

(3) _____. Vicros can fight but prefers to direct the Chosen from the shadows and safety of the Ruins of Pine Hollow Keep. He's ambitious, subtle and (4) _____.

1. "Charlatan," "True believer" or you pick something else based on a player's goal.

If your party contains a character with **Goal E** related to the Chosen, then Vicros is a charlatan who has stolen someone else's identity. Decide now who Vicros really is, preferably someone important to the character with **Goal E**, and record it here: ____

_____

_____

2. This is the powerful lieutenant for the player(s) with **Goal G** related to the Chosen. Ask the respective players now about who they wish to slay and why, and record it here: _____

_____

_____

If no one in your party has this goal, just use Zuzar (below) as a placeholder for now.

3. This is the missing family member of the player(s) with **Goal F** related to the Chosen. Ask those players now who they are trying to rescue and why, and record it here: _____

_____

_____

If no one in your party has this goal, create a prominent local craftsman to fill this role for now.

4. Decide on a last adjective for Vicros depending on how villainous you want him to be and how he fits into your game. If your players' goals are about justice and righteousness, they might do well with a sadistic or cruel villain, but players looking to make a quick buck might do better with a more conniving or brutally capitalist villain.

Vicros needs mid- and short-term goals that overlap with player goals, so we'll first choose long-term goals for him that concern the same people, places and objects as the player goals do. If your party contains a character with...

Goal D: Vicros wants the same item and believes it is in Ivrut's hoard. You can decide later why Vicros wants it.

Goal B: Vicros wants to learn the same spell and believes it is in Ivrut's hoard (even if it is not). You can decide later why Vicros wants to learn it.

Neither: Vicros believes he can lift the enchantment on the dragon hoard and claim the powerful items there for himself.

Vicros's long-term goals align very simply with his faction's goals here, but in your game, you may wish to make his long-term goals more specific to your characters.

Finally, we'll create short-term goals for Vicros that are based on his long-term goal of unearthing the buried hoard of Ivrut.

No matter which goals your party is following, Vicros will be directing his cultists to dig in the Abandoned Mineshaft to locate the cavern where Ivrut used to lair. Vicros is also looking to hire muscle to defend the miners from Those Left Behind and to keep the BMTC off the mountain.

If your party contains a character with **Goal H** related to the Chosen, Vicros is also trying to convert some of the locals to his dragon cult with his weekly sermons in town.

ZUZAR

Zuzar is a devoted member of the Chosen of Ivrut, being a dragonborn descendant of Ivrut herself (or so she claims). Zuzar is a fearsome fighter and former gladiator whose past victories include (1) _____. Zuzar has been by Vicros's side for the past few years and has been a (2) _____ lieutenant to the cult's leader. Zuzar aims to reclaim the dragon hoard she believes is her birthright, including (3) _____.

1. Some past crimes. If one of your players has **Goal G** related to the Chosen, Zuzar is their target. Ask the player why their character wants to slay Zuzar and make this past victory related to that. If your player wants to slay Zuzar for money (if they want to play a bounty hunter or something similar), decide who is paying them to slay Zuzar and have that be part of Zuzar's past victory instead. If no one in your party has **Goal G** related to the Chosen, then establish that Zuzar slew a prince's beloved gladiator in the ring and had to skip town.

2. "Loyal" or "treacherous." If one of your players has **Goal E** related to the Chosen, have Zuzar be distrustful of Vicros and willing to work toward deposing him and assuming control of the cult. Otherwise, have Zuzar be a loyal follower like the rest.

3. This is the item from **Goal D** for a player that chose to relate the goal to the Chosen. If none of your players have this goal, Zuzar seeks a preserved dragon egg rumored to be in the hoard: a little sibling for Zuzar to raise.

For this game, we'll assume Zuzar's long-term goal aligns with her faction and she wishes to unearth the buried hoard of Ivrut. Some of the information above may change her motives for seeking this hoard, but she'll help the faction work toward finding it regardless.

Now, we'll create short-term goals for Zuzar that relate to how she pursues her long-term goal.

- Zuzar has been tasked by Vicros with defending the mineshaft excavation from Those Left Behind and BMTC prospectors. Since she's also interested in finding the hoard, she stays close to the excavation and oversees the cultists as they work to unearth it.

- If a player has **Goal D** relating to an item in the hoard of Ivrut, Zuzar also wants that item and her goal is to take that item from the hoard for herself, by force if necessary.

JENNVA FAROVEN

Jennva Faroven is a dwarven geomancer, prospector and adventurer who is in charge of the BMTC's prospecting expedition in Pine Hollow. She (1) _____ the rumors of a dragon hoard under the mountain. While Jennva is the leader of the expedition, she doesn't have a great deal of authority over the rank-and-file miners in the BMTC, and (2) _____. She directly commands a squad of dwarven geomancers, including (3) _____ and a few others with close ties to her family. Jennva is a powerful spellcaster and is capable of kick-starting a mining operation by blowing the top off of a mountain, provided she has time for preparation, a good crew and access to (4) _____. Before she was a member of the BMTC, she was (5) _____.

1. "Believes" or "does not believe". If your party contains a character with **Goal B** or **Goal D** related to the Lost Hoard of Ivrut, Jennva believes the rumors and is interested in finding the hoard as well. Otherwise, she dismisses the rumors.

2. "Wants to expand control" or "doesn't". If your party contains a member with **Goal H** related to the BMTC, Jennva wants more control over miners. If no one in your party has such a goal, she doesn't care.

3. This is the powerful lieutenant for the player(s) with **Goal G** related to the BMTC. Ask the respective players about who they wish to slay and why, and record the name here: _____

If no one in your party has this goal, use Darmil as a placeholder.

4. This is the location listed in **Goal A** or **Goal C**. Jennva needs access to this location to perform a geomancy ritual.

If no one in your party has this goal, use the Ruins of Pine Hollow Keep instead.

5. If your party contains a player with **Goal E** related to the BMTC, decide who Jennva was before joining (preferably someone important to the player) and record it here: _____

If no one in your party has this goal, Jennva was a black market gemstone dealer.

Jennva needs mid- and short-term goals that overlap with the players' goals, so we'll first choose long-term goals for her that concern the same people, places and objects as the player goals do. If your party contains a character with...

Goal F: Jennva has exaggerated the riches buried in the mountain and convinced the family member from this goal to join the BMTC.

If Jennva believes in the rumors of Ivrut's hoard, she wants to find the hoard before beginning mining operations, since her destructive mining methods could make the hoard difficult or impossible to access.

This means that Jennva's long-term goals might differ based on your party's goals. Jennva either aims to find the lost hoard of Ivrut while pretending to prospect, or she simply wants to blow the top off the mountain to start mining. Decide which goal she is pursuing and record it here:_____

Now we'll need to formulate mid- and short-term goals based on that long-term goal.

• If Jennva is searching for the hoard, she'll need to seize control of the Collapsed Mineshaft from the Chosen.

• To access the mineshaft, Jennva might look for a back way in.

• Blowing the top off the mountain requires a geomancy ritual that Jennva knows, requiring eight runes to be carved in certain places in the mountain, to form a larger glyph. Five have been drawn.

If Jennva wants to start mining operations right away, she'll need to seize control of the location listed in (4) on pg. 211 first.

DARMIL FAROVEN

Darmil Faroven is Jennva's younger brother. He joined the BMTC before her but was placed under her command and still resents it. Darmil (1) _____ the rumors about Ivrut's hoard buried under the mountain. A talented prospector, Darmil commands a crew of hard-working miners, including (2) _____. Darmil is certain he can surpass his sister in the BMTC's estimation if he can learn the secret of (3) _____.

1. Darmil believes the opposite of whatever Jennva believes.

2. The missing family member from **Goal F** on pg. 206 for players who chose that goal related to the BMTC. Ask your player(s) with this goal who they are seeking and record it here:_____

_____

Because Darmil opposes his sister, his function in your game will be the opposite of Jennva's. If she ends up as an ally to the players, he will be an antagonist; if she is their enemy, he is a useful ally. Your group's attitudes toward both of these characters may change as the adventure unfolds, so give Darmil a dramatic face or heel turn to oppose Jennva if her allegiances change.

Darmil's long-term goal is to uncover the lost hoard of Ivrut or blow the top off the mountain to start mining operations, whichever goal Jennva does not have.

Because we want Darmil to be a wild card, we'll have a rare case of an NPC whose goals might not align with his faction's. Determine his mid-term goal and record it here: _____

THRUNDIR FORGEGLOW

An amiable dwarf who loves to chat but is hard of hearing, Thrundir is the only priest at the only chapel in town, which happens to be devoted to (1) _____. Thrundir is a priest, not a cleric, but occasionally minor lucky things happen to him, which he calls "blessings." Thrundir has lived in Pine Hollow his whole life and is concerned about the recent influence of (2) _____ in town. He will talk about this to anyone who will listen.

1. The patron deity of your most religious party member, unless that's inappropriate for some reason. If no one in your party is religious, choose the dwarf god of civilization and/or the earth in your setting.

2. Either the BMTC or the Chosen, whichever your party is more opposed to (if the goals concerning those factions are connected, Thrundir sides with the most religious PC).

Thrundir's long-term goal is to drive both the BMTC and the Chosen out of town. He's concerned about the ecological devastation that blowing the top off the mountain might cause and about cult members recruiting townspeople and making them work without pay. If appropriate, Thrundir wrote to the most religious PC and explicitly asked for aid with his goal.

CREATING LOCATIONS

Now that we have factions whose goals overlap with the PCs' goals and NPCs whose goals align with or oppose them, we'll start to prepare for encounter design. First, we'll create some locations where these goals are likely to be completed.

THE RUINS OF PINE HOLLOW KEEP

An imposing structure of square stones charred to black by dragonfire, the Ruins of Pine Hollow Keep were once a nigh-impenetrable fortress built to protect the bountiful goods of the mines before they were shipped downriver. The great dragon Ivrut slew the inhabitants long ago and absconded with most of the treasure, but the Chosen of Ivrut have since taken up residence within its crumbling halls. The ruins still hold their share of defenses, and some locals say the dragon didn't take all the treasure.

The Ruins of Pine Hollow Keep are located on the opposite side of the river from Pine Hollow and are currently occupied by the Chosen of Ivrut. The defending forces are led by (1) _____

_____. The vaults are mostly empty, having been cleared out by Ivrut, and the cult hasn't managed to open them—yet. The vaults aren't totally empty, however, since Ivrut left behind things they had no use for, including (2) _____.

1. The Chosen lieutenant named by the player with **Goal G** related to the Chosen. If no player has this goal, this is Vicros.

2. The spell chosen by the player with **Goal B** related to this location or the magic item chosen by the player with **Goal D** related to this location. If no player has this goal, the vault contains the spell Darmil seeks.

COLLAPSED MINESHAFT

Long ago lost to earthquakes and age, this ancient series of mineshafts contains mounds of raw, unextracted ore, as well as abandoned minecart rails, pulleys and a multitude of equipment. Those Left Behind skitter through the darkness, occasionally clawing their way through the rubble to wreak havoc on the surface.

The mineshaft is located near the Ruins of Pine Hollow Keep, and an old minecart track still runs from the tunnel entrance to the gates of the keep through a narrow rocky pass. The lower-ranking Chosen, including (1) _____, are excavating the old caved-in tunnels here. The excavation is being overseen by (2) _____, who keeps an eye on the darkness at all times, waiting for the next attack by Those Left Behind.

1. The family member identified by the player with **Goal F** related to the Chosen. If no player has this goal, a few locals have joined the Chosen and are working here.

2. The Chosen lieutenant identified by the player with **Goal G** related to the Chosen, plus Zuzar. If no player has this goal, the only overseer is Zuzar.

PINE HOLLOW

A rough and tumble town far from most civilization, Pine Hollow used to be the center of a massive ore-extracting operation. Now the BMTC hopes it can find new treasure buried in the mountain. Dozens of migrants have arrived hoping to strike it rich by working for the BMTC. Vendors populate the dirt streets of the small settlement peddling a wide variety of wares.

The town of Pine Hollow is the base of operations for both the BMTC and the Council and is located opposite the ruins. The defending forces are led by (1)_____, keeping an eye out for interlopers hoping to claim the wealth within. This is also where (2)_____, an active member of the community on behalf of the BMTC, can most often be found.

1. If a player has taken **Goal G** in relation to the BMTC, the forces are led by that figure. If no players have this goal, the BMTC in the area are led by Jennva herself.

2. If a player has taken **Goal F** in relation to the BMTC, that family member has taken a position here. If no player has this goal, several new arrivals hoping to strike it rich have joined up instead.

THE DUSTY CUP

A charming three-story inn that stands out for having been built more recently than everything else in town, the Dusty Cup serves both as a nexus for trade and activity and a fortified base for the BMTC. Though it appears modest, the base construction is solid, and the unassuming guards have a few magical tricks up their sleeves.

The Dusty Cup is a rough-and-tumble place filled with members of the BMTC after a long day's work. It's packed with (1)_____, which is used to maintain a sense of security. This is also the area where (2)_____ is most frequently found.

1. If a player has **Goal C** in hopes to take the Tavern, the place is filled with defensive gear: solid walls, armor, shields and weapons. If no player has this goal, the Tavern is instead filled with mining gear and copious amounts of drink.

2. If a player has **Goal G** in relation to the BMTC, that lieutenant is here. Otherwise, the figure is Jennva.

THE CHAPEL OF REST

An old chapel near the edge of town, tucked in between the back of a cluster of cottages and an abandoned mill. The chapel was built to honor the deities of the dwarven pantheon, but now the priest who tends the place determines who is venerated here.

This chapel is dedicated to Thrundir Forgeglow's primary deity. As the priest of this chapel, Thrundir lives here, but few come to pray. After Thrundir meets the party in the first encounter, he offers to let them stay on a few cots in the chapel. The location at the edge of town and quiet atmosphere make it an ideal resting place. When players take a long rest here, they gain 2d10 temporary hit points, which can take them over their usual maximum. If they offend Thrundir, or for some reason are no longer worthy of it, it fades at the next sunset.

THE LOST HOARD OF IVRUT

Deep in the mountain, an ancient cavern supported by old dwarven mining structures survived the dragon's attack. Here, Ivrut piled the wealth of the mountain. Later, when Ivrut was driven from its lair by an unknown beast from the depths, the hoard was abandoned, protected by powerful draconic magic. Whatever drove the dragon away left the treasure behind.

According to rumor, the hoard is buried deep beneath the mountain and will only be found when (1) _____, or some other brave soul, uncovers it. The hoard is said to hold some rare and forgotten treasures, including (2) _____.

1. The Chosen, or the BMTC if Jennva believes the hoard is real and wants to find it.

2. The spell from **Goal B** and/or the magic item from **Goal D**, if your party has players with these goals related to this location.

PREPARING FOR CONFLICT

We have the NPCs your characters will meet and the locations where they'll clash, so now we can move on to creating the information we'll need to run combat encounters. We've created 5e stat blocks for the main threats you'll face. Work through each stat block and decide what tweaks need to be made based on your party's goals. Suggestions are provided as a guideline under "Stat Changes."

VICROS DRAKEBLOOD

If Vicros is a true believer, he fights viciously and to the death. He kills as many enemies as possible and offers no mercy unless he is offered some greater way to serve Ivrut. If Vicros is a charlatan, he preserves his own hide above all else. He takes a knife to any creature that drops to 0 hit points and attempts to negotiate and uses his goons as distractions to cover his own escape.

ZUZAR

Zuzar is a fanatical believer who does everything she can to uphold the will of her masters. Her fighting style is aggressive—she prioritizes whoever she perceives to be the strongest. If a player is linked to her through a past crime, she prioritizes them instead if such action makes sense in the story.

Zuzar is a cult fanatic (SRD) with an additional 20 hit points and the additional action:

> **Ivrut's Exalted Exhalation (Recharge 6):** Zuzar breathes draconic fire in a 15-foot cone. Each creature in this area must succeed on a DC 11 Dexterity saving throw or take 14 (4d6) fire damage or half as much on a successful save. The terrain in this

VICROS DRAKEBLOOD

Medium humanoid (half-elf), chaotic evil

Armor Class 12 (15 with *mage armor*)
Hit Points 82 (11d8 + 33)
Speed 30 ft.

STR	DEX	CON	INT	WIS	CHA
10 (+0)	14 (+2)	16 (+3)	10 (+0)	11 (+0)	16 (+3)

Mad Devotion (3/Day). Once per turn when Vicros Drakeblood fails a saving throw, he may take 4 (2d4) psychic damage to reroll the save.

Spellcasting. Vicros Drakeblood is an 8th-level spellcaster. His spellcasting ability is Charisma (spell save DC 14, +6 to hit with spell attacks). Vicros has the following sorcerer spells prepared:

Cantrips (at will): *dancing lights, fire bolt, prestidigitation*
1st level (4 slots): *burning hands, mage armor, shield*
2nd level (3 slots): *hold person, scorching ray, suggestion*
3rd level (3 slots): *fear, fireball*
4th level (2 slots): *polymorph, wall of fire*

ACTIONS

Multiattack. Vicros casts one spell and uses Ivrut's Exalted Exhalation if available.

Ivrut's Exalted Exhalation. Vicros breathes fire in a 15-foot cone. Each creature in that area must succeed on a DC 14 Dexterity saving throw or take 24 (7d6) fire damage on a failed save or half as much on a successful one. The terrain in this cone is set ablaze for 1 minute, and any creature that begins its turn in the flames or enters that area for the first time on its turn takes 6 (2d6) fire damage.

Dagger. Melee or Ranged Weapon Attack: +5 to hit, reach 5 ft. or range 20/60 ft., one target. *Hit:* 4 (1d4 + 2) piercing damage.

BONUS ACTIONS

All Consuming. As a Bonus Action, Vicros magically causes any active fires within 30 feet of himself, including those caused by Ivrut's Exalted Exaltation, to spread 5 feet in all directions.

REACTIONS

Burn It All. When Vicros is subjected to a critical hit, he may immediately use Ivrut's Exalted Exaltation as a reaction if available. If unavailable, he instead regains his use of the feature.

GM NOTE: STAT CHANGES

If Vicros is a charlatan as a result of a player choosing **Goal E**, he instead conjures illusory dragon's breath that only appears to be massive flames. It functions similarly as before, except it prompts an Intelligence saving throw and deals psychic damage instead of fire.

cone is set ablaze for 1 minute, and any creature that begins its turn in the flames or moves there for the first time on its turn takes 3 (1d6) fire damage.

GM NOTE: STAT CHANGES

If a player hopes to slay Zuzar as a result of Goal G, her past crimes have given her an edge in battle. She gains an additional ability:

Dirty Trick. When a creature fails a saving throw or is hit by a spell from Zuzar, she may use Ivrut's Exalted Exhalation as a bonus action if it is available. If it is not available, she regains a use of the feature.

JENNVA FAROVEN

Jennva Faroven is a cunning combatant, striking what she perceives to be weak points. If she is a believer in the Hoard of Ivrut, she is more easily manipulated when wealth and power are dangled in front of her nose.

DARMIL FAROVEN

Darmil does the opposite of whatever his sister does. If she accepts bribes, he is moral and virtuous. If she is a cunning fighter, he is reckless and bold.

Darmil is a veteran (SRD) with the following changes:

Geomancer: Darmil cannot be knocked prone against his will while touching solid stone.

Foreman's Command (Recharge 6): As a bonus action, Darmil may command one ally within 30 feet to make a single weapon attack as a reaction.

Stat Changes: If Darmil is a potential ally to the players (i.e., they oppose his sister) he uses the stats above. If he is more likely to be an enemy, he loses his Foreman's Command ability and instead

JENNVA FAROVEN

Medium humanoid (human), lawful neutral

Armor Class 17 (breastplate, shield)
Hit Points 97 (13d8 + 39)
Speed 30 ft., climb 30 ft.

STR	DEX	CON	INT	WIS	CHA
16 (+3)	13 (+3)	16 (+3)	16 (+3)	12 (+1)	13 (+1)

Saving Throws Str +6, Cha +4
Skills Arcana +6, Nature +6, Perception +4, Persuasion +4, Survival +4
Senses tremorsense 30 ft., passive Perception 14
Languages Common, Terran
Challenge 6 (2,300 XP)

Innate Spellcasting. Jennva's innate spellcasting ability is Intelligence (spell save DC 14, +6 to hit with spell attacks). She can cast the following spells, using her hammer as a spellcasting focus:

At will: *grease, thunderwave*
3/day each: *hold person, slow*
1/day: *wall of stone*

ACTIONS

Multiattack. Jennva makes two Warhammer attacks. She may replace one attack with a spell.
Warhammer. Melee Weapon Attack: +6 to hit, reach 5 ft., one target. *Hit:* 7 (1d8 + 3) bludgeoning damage or 8 (1d10 + 3) bludgeoning damage if used with two hands.

BONUS ACTIONS

Earth Shake. Jennva stomps the ground, causing it to shake. All creatures within 10 feet of her must succeed on a DC 14 Strength saving throw or fall prone.

GM NOTE: STAT CHANGES

If Jennva believes in the Hoard of Ivrut (from **Goal B** or **D**) she gains:

Enthralled by Gold. Jennva is immune to the charmed condition except when it is inflicted by a member of the Chosen of Ivrut. She also has disadvantages against saving throws prompted by members of that faction.

If she does not believe in the hoard, she instead gains:

Tough Mind. Jennva may add her Constitution modifier (+3) to Intelligence and Wisdom saving throws.

instead gains the action:

Swallowed by Stone (Recharge 6): Every creature standing on stone within 30 feet of Darmil must succeed on a DC 13 Strength saving throw or be grappled as they sink partially into the stone beneath their feet. They remain grappled until they break free by repeating the save as an action or by dealing at least 10 points of damage to the stone in a single hit (AC 15).

THOSE LEFT BEHIND SKULKER

Medium humanoid (goblinoid), chaotic evil

Armor Class 16 (hide armor, shield)
Hit Points 27 (5d8 + 5)
Speed 30 ft., climb 30 ft.

STR	DEX	CON	INT	WIS	CHA
14 (+2)	15 (+2)	13 (+1)	8 (-1)	11 (+0)	9 (-1)

Skills Stealth +6, Survival +2
Senses darkvision 120 ft., passive Perception 10
Languages Common, Goblin
Challenge 1 (200 XP)

Spider Climb. The skulker can climb difficult surfaces, including upside down on ceilings, without needing to make ability checks.
Sunlight Sensitivity. While in sunlight, the skulker has disadvantage on attack rolls as well as Wisdom (Perception) rolls that rely on sight.

ACTIONS

Multiattack. The skulker makes one Greatclub attack and one Grapple check. If the skulker is grappling a creature, it may instead make two Dagger attacks against that creature.
Greatclub. Melee Weapon Attack: +4 to hit, reach 5 ft., one target. *Hit:* 6 (1d8 + 2) bludgeoning damage.
Dagger. Melee or Ranged Weapon Attack: +4 to hit, reach 5 ft. or range 20/60 ft., one target. *Hit:* 4 (1d4 + 2) piercing damage.

BONUS ACTIONS

Back to the Shadows. The skulker may take the Hide action as a Bonus Action while in dim light or darkness.

THOSE LEFT BEHIND

The inhabitants of the mines strike from the shadows, latching onto foes and stabbing them repeatedly. If they're thrown off, they skitter back to the shadows and reposition to attack again.

CREATING REWARDS

As your players pursue their goals, they'll expect to reap the rewards of their efforts. In addition to experience rewards and the treasure you'd like to bestow for defeating enemies, each completed goal should reward the player who completed it. Below are rewards, per character, for completing the eight goals listed in the Character Goal Generation section.

Code	Reward
Goal A	Control of the area's defenses, plus unofficial legal ownership of the area, at least until the real owner comes by to collect.
Goal B	The player learns the new spell and always has it prepared without it counting against their total prepared spells.
Goal C	Possession of the area's resources and treasures, plus unofficial legal ownership of the area, at least until the real owner comes by to collect.
Goal D	The magic item, plus a level-appropriate treasure hoard.
Goal E	Knowledge of the true identity of the faction leader, plus evidence they murdered the person whose name they now use.
Goal F	The family member agrees to leave with them and reveals they have stolen a level-appropriate treasure hoard from the faction before leaving.
Goal G	Proof they slew the lieutenant, plus the +1 weapon the lieutenant carried.
Goal H	Membership in the faction, plus access to the faction's general supplies.

DESIGNING ENCOUNTERS

It's finally time to put all the pieces together and design some encounters for the adventures your party will have in Pine Hollow. We've provided a few example encounters below, based on the encounters our group ran into during playtesting. You can tweak these to fit your party or create your own using the steps in Chapter 7.

THE CULT RECRUITS NEW MEMBERS

In the middle of the day, when Jennva Faroven is prospecting out on the mountain, Vicros visits the town square outside the Dusty Cup with a dozen cultists. He stands on an overturned wheelbarrow and stokes the passions of the out-of-work miners, trying to persuade them to join his cause. Nearby, Darmil Faroven leans against a barrel and watches, muttering under his breath.

• Vicros attempts to persuade the miners, frustrated that they're waiting to get started, to join him in his goal (whatever that is in your game).

• If the players don't take action, Darmil Faroven attacks Vicros and tries to rally the miners to his side instead.

• In a fair fight, Vicros defeats Darmil and kills him (at GM discretion). If the players interfere, anything is possible.

• If Vicros succeeds in recruiting others (which he will unless the players interfere, even if he has to kill Darmil first), advance his excavation-related goal. If he is frustrated, leave it alone for a day or two as he regroups. If he is killed, leave it alone for several days as the cult regroups under Zuzar's leadership.

JENNVA GETS FED UP

On one of her trips out to the mountainside to carve blasting runes, Jennva Faroven catches the party following her and confronts them violently. Using her geomancy abilities, she attempts to trap and subdue them with stone so she can interrogate them about the Chosen's plans (even if the players aren't allied with the Chosen—she's paranoid).

- Jennva uses her geomancy to trap the players in a box of solid stone walls with her personal guards, all dwarven veterans (SRD).
- This is a close-quarters fight where swinging weapons is impractical. The veterans will attack with their fists and try to subdue the party alive, until one of the party draws steel—then it gets deadly.
- If Jennva's guards are defeated, she will leave the party trapped within the *wall of stone* (see those rules for escaping) and attempt to flee. She won't fight them again without a clear advantage. Through sheer personal animosity, she might retaliate against the Cult, even mistakenly.

SHADOWY WHISPERS

Zuzar, accompanied or trailed by the PCs, ventures into the mines below the mountain in hopes of finding the vault or weaknesses in enemy defenses. While traveling, the group is found and attacked by Those Left Behind.

- Those Left Behind do everything in their power to keep the area dark, retreating to the shadows and surprising their foes.
- The narrow tunnels allow Those Left Behind to attack targets one-on-one—they prefer to grapple and stab their opponents

over a fair fight.

• Those Left Behind flee when close to death, but if captured, they can barely speak coherently. They take no prisoners.

• If Zuzar makes it through Those Left Behind, she finds the weakness she's after—this could be a prime place for a geomancy rune, an excellent route straight to Pine Hollow or even a path to Ivrut's Hoard.

MAGICAL SABOTAGE

One of the geomancy runes carved into the mountainside by Jennva in preparation for blasting has been discovered by local **kobolds** (SRD), who see it as an omen of Ivrut's return. They have set up a small shrine around it in the days since Jennva carved it.

• A group of kobolds (or other appropriate cave-dwellers) is worshiping at the rune, which has been magically chiseled into the stone. Half of them are non-combatants but the others are armed with old mining equipment.

• If confronted, the armed kobolds will cover the escape of the unarmed ones back up into the trees. After half of the armed kobolds are defeated, the rest will flee and hide in their lair, behind numerous traps.

• The kobold lair is dug into an old mineshaft, so if the players follow them and discover it, they find a back way into the mineshaft and access to the dig site.

CULT DOWN TO SIZE

If the players decide to attack the old keep, or if the BMTC does, the cult will defend itself with deadly force. They are willing to destroy the fort to defeat their enemies but will defend the dig site the fort grants access to with a fanatical devotion. Vicros joins the fray if things are going badly for the defenders.

- The old keep has only three intact walls. The broken fourth wall has been patched with rubble and logs.

- Defenders lob stones and alchemist's fire from the walls, but the other defenses aren't working: The cult relies on its numbers and the devotion of the faithful to win.

- If the fort looks lost, the cult may detonate their remaining stores of alchemist's fire to deter the attackers, then retreat to the Collapsed Mineshaft to regroup. If Vicros and Zuzar are both defeated, they flee instead.

- Remember, control of the fort means control of the path to the mineshaft, so any faction who wishes to dig for the hoard must control it.

Battle for the Dragon's Hoard

After the brutal trials to the hoard, it's finally within reach...if only the party can get past the opposition in the way, outside a massive vault door.

- The final battle changes depending on the main opposition of the PCs—either Vicros Drakeblood or Jennva Faroven.

- The goals of both players and enemies may change the nature of the fight—the battle may be to the death, or the magic item may be used by the adversary.

- When defeated, a true believer in the hoard likely fights to the death, but anyone else is likely willing to flee instead.

RUNNING THE GAME

If you've been following along, you already have all the prep you need to start this game. Otherwise, gather your players and work through the goals together. Walk them through the premise of the game and discuss the goals each character will have.

As your players decide on their goals, you can scan through the NPCs and Locations sections and make the tweaks you need to make the game your own. Fill in the blanks on the description for each NPC or location to adapt the adventure to your table, and make sure to add any additional notes you need to keep track of. Take a moment to review the stat blocks presented in the combat section and note the changes in the enemy abilities and tactics that might appear in your game. Also, review the rewards section and clarify with your players what certain open-ended rewards (like the powerful spell from **Goal B**) entail.

Finally, organize all the information you need on the cheat sheet that follows. This should contain everything you need to keep track of the game as it develops. You'll notice that the faction goals have already been filled in since no matter how your NPCs and location develop, the faction goals will stay the same. Each one is printed with a few things that might happen to advance the clock, but you should advance the clock whenever you think the narrative calls for it (see pg. 73 for suggestions).

Many players will want to start by seeking out information: consider the cheat sheet's list of faction and NPC goals to be your rumor table, and when players gather information, reward them with insight and additional actionable information.

When the players are done and your cheat sheet is filled out, it's time to start the game. Begin by reading the introduction below, or introduce your players to the game in your own way.

If you follow the Brasscrown River north, up into the hills, you'll leave civilization behind. Through the pines, up over the granite walls of the river canyon and nestled in a hollow near the wild part of the mountain lies the town of Pine Hollow. You've all arrived here together after a week on the road, and you're eager for a meal and some proper rest. As you come up over the hill, you see the town below. Smoke rises from a few chimneys, but the town is quiet in the afternoon.

Next, you'll need to set the stage with additional details about the factions and locations the party is likely to run into. Read the paragraph in the Setting section, followed by the paragraphs you created for each NPC and each location. Assume that characters share enough information with each other that the whole party knows everything you read.

If your players like to set the scene with some roleplaying, try placing the characters in a social mindset and ask them a few of the questions from Chapter 7 as they walk into town. For example:

1. Which character in the party do you trust the most? The least?
2. What is the greatest adventure you've ever been on?
3. What is your morning routine like?
4. Have you ever seen a dragon? How did that change you?
5. Why are we heading to Pine Hollow anyway?

Once the players are situated, it's time to throw them into the first encounter. After that, encourage them to take the reins and pursue their goals all throughout Pine Hollow and the surrounding area. When you're ready, get started like this:

As you reach the edge of town, your boots hit something hard under the packed dirt. There used to be cobblestones here, long ago, but they've been stamped down under layer after layer of packed dust. Up ahead, you see a plume of dirt being kicked up and hear a commotion from the other side of a low stone building. As you round the corner, you see people fighting in the dirt and a small crowd of onlookers cheering them on. One of the brawlers is (1) _____ and the other is (2) _____. An old dwarf in priest's robes is marching towards them with an angry look on his face, shouting for them to cut it out.

1. Describe the appearance of the enemy lieutenant from **Goal G** here, or describe Darmil if no one in your group has **Goal G**. If more than one player has **Goal G**, choose the enemy less likely to be killed on the spot.

2. If you have a player in your party with **Goal F** related to the opposite faction as the player with **Goal G** above, describe the appearance of the missing family member here. Otherwise, describe a rank-and-file member of the faction opposite as the one above.

These two brawlers are fighting over an imagined slight. Someone bumped someone else on the street, and tensions are so high that it broke out into violence. The onlookers belong to both factions and are itching to get in on the action. Only Thrundir Forgeglow's presence is stopping the fight from becoming rowdier, as he tries to separate the two and get them to take it out of the town.

Remember that a player with **Goal C** already knows about Thrundir, and religious PCs might have already corresponded with him, but might not know him on sight. The player with **Goal G** might not know their target on sight, either. The player with **Goal F** probably knows their target on sight. Try to use this as an opportunity for the characters to speak with a faction representative and learn from them.

RUNNING PROACTIVE PUBLISHED ADVENTURES

We should mention here that our preference is to run our own adventures set in our own world, rather than running a published adventure. In a published adventure, it's assumed characters will care about certain (pre-written) things and act in certain (predictable) ways. If your players are on board, you can just ask them to have their characters take on those goals, and run a published adventure in a proactive way as the characters follow those goals from the "intro hooks" section of the adventure.

With a flexible and experienced group, this works fine. But if you're having trouble, consider adapting a published adventure instead of using it word-for-word. You can use the locations, loot tables, villains and monsters to great effect if you tweak their motivations and the sequence of events to fit the player goals you've already established. Of course, if you have the time to plan and the confidence to improvise, we find that proactive fantasy is best in a world of your group's creation rather than a published setting. If you'd like to work with an example of how to adapt a published adventure to this style of play, this adventure is a great template to get you started.

This adventure is set in a simple setting of our design, but we walk you through how to adapt it to the goals of your group. It's designed to be a good introduction to how our system works in practice, so we highly encourage you to actually run it instead of just reading it. —*JF*

CHEAT SHEET

FACTION GOALS

An easy-to-organize space to keep track of goals

The Chosen of Ivrut: Excavate the way to the Lost Hoard of Ivrut

Brasscrown Mountain Trading Company: Complete the geomancy ritual and blow the top off the mountain

Ivrut   *Brasscrown*

Vicros Drakeblood

Goal 1: _____

Goal 2: _____

Jennva Faroven

Goal 1: _____

Goal 2: _____

Zuzar

Goal 1: _____

Goal 2: _____

Darmil

Goal 1: _____

Goal 2: _____

Thrundir Forgeglow

Goal 1: _____

Goal 2: _____

GOAL CLOCKS

Once you know what they're after, use these clocks to track each NPC's progress.

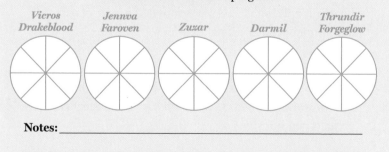

Vicros Drakeblood   *Jennva Faroven*   *Zuzar*   *Darmil*   *Thrundir Forgeglow*

Notes: _____

_____

PLAYER GOALS

Player A*:* _____

Player B: _____

Player C: _____

Player D: _____

Player E: _____

SUGGESTED ADVENTURE ROADMAP
A step-by-step guide to your story

1. First Encounter *street brawl at the edge of town*

2. Introduce Thrundir *and the Chapel of Rest, or your game's equivalent*

4a. Players Discover the Lost Hoard... *(run encounters for players to achieve Goal A or C)...*

3. Players Pursue Goals *and learn about the two main factions (run encounters for players to achieve Goals E, F, G and H)*

4b. ...or the Faction Achieves Its Goals *and discovers the hoard*

5. Players Fight to Control the Hoard *in the final encounter of the adventure (Goal B or D)*

6. Establish Consequences *that will spark future goals (suggestion: the return of Ivrut)*

AFTERWORD

WHEN THE FIRST BOOK in the *Game Master* series (*The Game Master's Book of Random Encounters*) was released, my hope was for it to become a tool GMs could use on the fly as their campaigns ran up against unexpected trouble due to player choices. As the series has grown in popularity, the focus of the books has expanded, as has its pool of contributors.

I had not intended to create a collection of resources that encourages proactive roleplaying, but in hindsight, I can see how each title in the *Game Master* series serves any GM seeking to establish a campaign informed by player goals instead of the traditional "bad guy does stuff, good guys try to stop him" pattern many TTRPG sourcebooks reinforce by default. Because all the *Game Master* books are primarily collections of plug-and-play encounter locations, skill challenge generators or adventure-inspiring character compendiums, they aren't bound by a narrative the players are forced to engage with.

For this reason, I'm thrilled the Fishel brothers expressed interest in publishing their guide to proactive roleplaying under the *Game Master* banner. The short-term goal of this afterword is to express my gratitude for their approach to the process of making the book as part of my mid-term goal: detailing the ways in which the philosophy of proactive roleplaying they've laid out has influenced the way I run my games. I love the premise of collaborative storytelling through TTRPGs. But as I get older and my hobbies and profession continue to merge, I'm finding it more difficult to session prep the way I used to. When I do put in the extra effort to sketch out possible campaign arcs for each of the players in my party, it often proves to be a waste of time because the players—the people meant to have autonomy with regard to their characters' actions—make choices I hadn't considered or ignore cleverly (or overtly) baited story hooks I'd placed in their path as they pursue things they actually care about. My games were full of people, places and things I was certain were intriguing enough to captivate my players, but I couldn't see the forest for the treants. My players wanted to do their own thing, pursue their own interests, become pirates or explore a wizard's archive or destroy a personal threat rather than focus on ridding the realm of an existential one.

As part of the process of putting this book together, I playtested its premises with my own parties and the results were staggering. I now have more time to develop the aspects of the game I care about while using those creations to play into (as opposed to against) my players' desires. They pursue the goals they've established for themselves and are therefore delighted at each session because every encounter is built around the things that matter to them. I no longer need to worry which path they'll pursue because they (or their stated goals) tell me where they're going. It's fantastic. And so simple. And only a little maddening since I didn't think of doing things this way at the outset.

The long-term goal of this afterword is to encourage you to incorporate as much or as little of the premise of proactive roleplaying into your games as you want. Even if you just reorient your campaign around player (as opposed to villain) goals, the power you're giving your players will free you up to more readily stand in their way.

The struggle to achieve a far-off aim is a major component of the hero's journey (the cornerstone of some of the most timeless tales in any genre). Why not make it the centerpiece of your own campaigns?

Jeff Ashworth
Author of *The Game Master's Book of Random Encounters*

ACKNOWLEDGMENTS

NEITHER OF US ARE AUTHORS and only one of us is a proper writer, so it is only due to a tremendous effort by other people that you are reading this at all. We'd like to thank Jeff Ashworth, the *Game Master* series author emeritus, for chatting with a stranger on Reddit and actually reading the manuscript we sent. We'd also like to thank Phil Sexton, who took a chance on us, and Tim Baker, whose patient attention to detail made this book readable. Additionally, we want to thank Courtney Kerrigan for her patience and flexibility with two bumbling never-authors.

Special thanks to Ginny Di for taking the time to read this book and write its foreword. We appreciate your kind words!

Thanks to our Blades in the Dark gaming group, which we assembled during the COVID-19 pandemic. That crew of rascals was always happy to talk about the philosophy of gaming after our sessions, and it's out of those conversations that the ideas in this book were born. In that vein, thanks to everyone who helped us work through and playtest these ideas, including but not limited to Alexander Blaha, Michael Wakefield, Andreas Moffett, Thompson Hangen, Sarah Fishel, Jessica Joyce, Dylan Kolhoff, Andrew Holtz, Andres Ponce, Will Theuer, Fletcher Travelstead, Hannah Scarlatoiu, Adam Tamrjan, Arman Fathi, Kyleigh Loy, Nicholas Kaplan, Jack Nowinski and Saarung Soomro.

ABOUT THE AUTHORS

JONAH FISHEL has been playing TTRPGs for nearly 20 years and has Game Mastered far more than his fair share of campaigns. Away from the gaming table, Jonah is a learning differences tutor. He lives in Durham, North Carolina with his wife, daughter and dog.

TRISTAN FISHEL is an author and RPG writer living in Newport News, Virginia. He's been playing TTRPGs for only slightly less time than his brother, having started his roleplaying career as a guinea pig for Jonah's dungeons. Tristan has written several adventures, rules expansions and other content for both 5e and a few of his other favored systems. In his spare time, Tristan enjoys running home games for his friends, writing fiction and serving as a devoted caretaker to his beloved cat, Cupcake.

GINNY DI is a Denver-based tabletop gaming YouTuber and cosplayer who loves telling stories, bringing characters to life and wearing the longest elf ears she can find. In addition to her self-published 5e adventures *Bard Behind Bars*, *The Cold and Hungry Sea* and *Flesh & Blood*, she creates downloadable 5e supplements for Patreon. Her game writing has been featured in *Potbellied Kobold's Guide to Villains & Lairs* from Jeff Stevens Games, *Battlezoo Ancestries: Dragons* from Roll for Combat and *Bardsung* and *Animal Adventures: The Faraway Sea* from Steamforged Games. On YouTube, she talks tabletop gaming etiquette and advice and explores character-building in games with music, skits and in-character roleplay videos that range from dramatic to comedic and invite the viewer to play along through the screen.

Media Lab Books
For inquiries, contact customerservice@topixmedia.com
Copyright 2023 Jonah Fishel and Tristan Fishel

Published by Topix Media Lab
14 Wall Street, Suite 3C
New York, NY 10005

Printed in China

ISBN-13: 978-1-956403-44-2
ISBN-10:1-956403-44-2

This work includes material taken from the System Reference Document 5.1 ("SRD 5.1") by Wizards of the Coast LLC and available at *https://dnd.wizards.com/resources/systems-reference-document*. The SRD 5.1 is licensed under the Creative Commons Attribution 4.0 International License available at *https://creativecommons.org/licenses/by/4.0/legalcode.*

1C-A24-2